THE PRACTICAL GUIDE TO A HEALTHY MARRIAGE

Step-by-Step Strategies for Lasting Happiness Through Effective Communication, Trust-Building Exercises, and Self-Care Practices

---

D.S. LODEN

Editing by The Pro Book Editor

1. Main category—Family and Relationships
2. Other category—Marriage and Long-Term Relationships

First Edition

Contents

Introduction

In a world filled with stories of love's highs and lows, the quest for a fulfilling marriage is universal. Despite their marriage vows to love each other forever, many couples need help maintaining their initial spark, hindered by misunderstandings and unmet expectations. This brings us to the core of most of the struggles in modern love and marriage.

This book stands out by recognizing the uniqueness of every marriage and every married person. It doesn't offer generic solutions; it is a tailored guide that respects the intricacies of each couple's journey. It presents an innovative blend of timeless principles and contemporary relationship dynamics, and it views technology as a tool for connection instead of a barrier.

At its heart, *The Practical Guide to a Healthy Marriage* is built on five key pillars:

1. effective communication,
2. trust-building,
3. deepening intimacy,
4. conflict resolution, and
5. fostering both personal and shared growth.

These pillars are brought to life through practical exercises, innovative strategies, and real-life case studies. This approach takes the intangible, the tangible, and the seemingly impossible into achievable realities.

My commitment to guiding couples through the intricacies of marriage stems from my own journey of transformative encounters, which showed me the profound impact of healthy relationship dynamics. We live in an unparalleled time when we face extraordinary challenges and stresses. This book is my heartfelt response to the modern challenges couples face, from juggling work-life demands to negotiating digital distractions and evolving gender roles. Each chapter is infused with this understanding and a genuine desire to help couples navigate the complexities of marriage in today's world.

I've written this book with deep respect for the diverse marital experiences and cultural diversity, ensuring every reader feels seen, understood, and supported. Whether you want to strengthen your bond, navigate through a rough patch, or better understand your partner, this user-friendly guide provides you with practical tools, step-by-step guides, personalized plans, and interactive workbook sections to ensure you are well-equipped to build a love that lasts a lifetime.

As we embark on this journey together, I invite you to walk this path as partners and individuals committed to growth, love, and understanding. The roadmap within these pages leads to a healthier marriage and a more satisfying partnership, beckoning with the promise of love's true potential unlocked.

As we begin, let us hold on to an unwavering optimism and empowerment, confident that while the journey to a fulfilling marriage requires effort, the rewards of a deepened, more satisfying partnership are not just a possibility—*they are within reach.*

ONE

Understanding Each Other's Communication Style

I n marriage, communication is crucial, but life's demands can make it hard to connect. Active listening is key to understanding unspoken messages. This chapter explores the art of active listening, which can transform conversations and strengthen the bond between partners.

The Art of Active Listening

Active listening is not just about waiting for your turn to speak or formulating a response while the other person is talking. The real challenge lies in making a significant shift from this reactive mode to a genuine, empathetic engagement. By doing so, you can overcome the instinct to prioritize internal thoughts or solutions and instead fully absorb and reflect on the speaker's emotions and intentions. This shift fosters deeper connection and mutual respect, essential for nurturing a healthy marriage.

Mirroring Techniques

One great way to enhance active listening is by mirroring your partner's words, but not by repeating them verbatim. Instead, you should try to rephrase their statements in your own words, much like a painter capturing the essence of a scene. By attentively absorbing your partner's message and then reflecting it back in a way that shows understanding and empathy, you can strengthen mutual understanding and deepen the emotional connection.

For instance, if your partner shares frustration about their day, you can respond with something like, "It seems like you had a tough day, and you're feeling overwhelmed." This validates their emotions, shows attentiveness, and helps deepen the emotional connection between you.

Defusing Conflicts with Empathy

The power of active listening lies in its ability to prevent conflicts from escalating by ensuring that both partners feel heard and valued. This approach helps to avoid misunderstandings and resentment.

Imagine a situation where tensions rise due to a misunderstanding about household responsibilities. Active listening offers a platform for both partners to express their perspectives without the fear of being dismissed. This paves the way for a solution that is rooted in mutual respect and understanding rather than contention. It transforms conflict into a collaborative problem-solving session, shifting the focus from winning the argument to better understanding and supporting each other.

Practical Exercises for Everyday Conversations

To encourage active listening in daily interactions, consider incorporating specific exercises that sharpen this skill. One such exercise involves dedicating a portion of your day to a distraction-free conversation during which you practice the techniques of complete presence, mirroring, and empathetic responses. During this time, turn off phones and other distractions and discuss anything significant to one or both of you. Ask clarifying questions without judgment, reflect on your partner's thoughts and feelings, and focus on truly understanding their perspective. This practice hones your active listening skills and reinforces the importance of your relationship, nurturing the bond you share.

Active listening is a dynamic process that evolves and deepens with practice. It requires patience, dedication, and a genuine desire to profoundly understand and connect with your partner. Married couples need to navigate the ups and downs of their shared journey with harmony and understanding. Learning to hear and truly listen creates a space where love and understanding flourish.

Decoding Non-Verbal Signals: Beyond Words

In the subtle dynamics of interpersonal communication, words are but the tip of the iceberg. Beneath the surface, many non-verbal signals play a crucial role, often conveying more meaning than spoken words ever can. Gestures, facial expressions, and posture form this silent language that, when interpreted, reveals the deeper layers of our partner's thoughts and emotions. Exploring this unspoken territory requires careful observation and understanding of human expression.

The dance of eyebrows, the cadence of a sigh, the silent eloquence of hands—these are the Morse code of our inner worlds, signaling sentiments that words may fail to capture. A furrowed brow may whisper worries; a slumped posture may echo exhaustion or defeat. Conversely, the light in one's eyes or a buoyant step can speak volumes about happiness and hope. When we recognize these cues, we tune in to a frequency that transcends verbal language and offers a glimpse into the unarticulated realms of feeling and thought that our partner inhabits.

Yet, as with any language, misinterpretations are common. A crossed arm may be read as defensiveness when, in reality, it's merely a quest for comfort. A misread sigh can be mistaken for exasperation rather than an expression of fatigue. These misinterpretations, innocent as they may seem, can seed misunderstandings that foster unnecessary conflict. It begs the question: how can one guide these waters with the precision of a skilled navigator, charting the course of true understanding without veering into the reefs of assumption?

The answer lies in the art of examination, a tool as potent as it is simple. Clarifying questions bridge the chasm of misunderstanding and allow us to verify our interpretations of these non-verbal messages. "You seem a bit quiet today. Is everything okay?"—such a question, posed with genuine curiosity, can open doors to conversations that might never have occurred. It signals to the partner that we are not merely passive observers of their emotional landscape but active participants, willing to venture into their inner world with empathy and openness.

To become more attuned to these non-verbal cues, one might adopt the stance of a detective, albeit one whose mission is to understand rather than solve a mystery. Noticing patterns in your partner's body language during different emotional states can provide valuable insights. How do they hold themselves when joyful, compared to when they're weighed down by sorrow? What silent signals do they send when they seek connection or, conversely, when they need space? Cataloging these observations, even mentally, sharpens our ability to read these cues in real-time and transforms our interactions into more unified mutual understanding.

Moreover, the context in which these non-verbal signals occur cannot be overstated. Depending on the situation, a touch, a glance, or a gesture might change its meaning entirely. Thus, a holistic approach is required—one that considers the environment, the preceding conversation, and even the day's events—as these factors can significantly influence the interpretation of non-verbal communication.

Engaging in exercises that heighten our sensitivity to non-verbal cues can further refine our abilities. One might, for instance, watch a muted film scene and try to infer the characters' emotions and intentions purely from their actions and expressions. Such exercises sharpen our observational skills and deepen our understanding of how humans communicate without words.

In essence, non-verbal communication is a multifaceted framework woven from the fibers of human emotion and expression. Deciphering this demands patience, attentiveness, and a willingness to ask questions that bridge the gap between perception and reality. By honing our ability to interpret these silent signals, we unlock a deeper connection with our partner, one that resonates with the profound understanding and empathy that lie at the heart of every lasting relationship.

The Power of Pause: Timing in Communication

In the dance of dialogue, the space between the steps—the pause—holds its own language, subtle yet profound in its ability to shape the conversation's flow. This silent beat, often overlooked in the rush to respond, stands as a guardian of understanding, granting both speaker and listener a moment to breathe, process, and reflect. In these silences, communication finds its depth, allowing for a response that is considered rather than reactive and for messages that are received with clarity rather than confusion.

Pausing before replying does more than just prevent the knee-jerk reactions that can derail dialogues; it signals respect. It shows that the words spoken are not merely heard but are being digested and pondered upon. This momentary halt in the exchange offers a sanctuary for thought, where the weight of the message can be measured and its implications understood. It's like a musician pausing between notes—not disrupting the melody but deepening its impact. The pause is a tool. When wielded with intention, it can transform the nature of conversations, turning exchanges fraught with potential misunderstanding into dialogues rich with empathy and insight.

Moreover, the strategic placement of pauses within a conversation can serve as a spotlight, drawing attention to the significance of what has been said or what is to come. It can underscore a point, signaling its importance without the need for embellishment. In moments where emotions run high, a well-timed pause can act as a buffer, a space where tempers can cool, and the precipice of escalation can be avoided. It's a subtle cue, one that invites reflection both in the speaker and the listener, fostering a dialogue that is more about understanding than rebuttal.

The impact of timing in communication extends beyond the immediate exchange; it influences how messages are perceived and absorbed. The rush to fill silence, to respond without delay, can often lead to words that are more about noise than meaning. In contrast, pausing for a moment of silence can imbue a conversation with a sense of gravity, encouraging both parties to engage more fully with the dialogue. It's a recognition that not all answers come readily and that the space between words can hold as much significance as the words themselves. Acknowledging this pause as a powerful communicative tool can elevate conversations, transforming them from simple exchanges of information into opportunities for authentic connection.

Incorporating pauses into dialogue requires mindfulness, a conscious effort to slow the pace of conversation, and to listen not just for the moment to speak but for the right moment to respond. Techniques to cultivate this practice can be as simple as adopting a mental count, a brief interlude before replying, allowing thoughts to settle and responses to form with clarity. It can involve actively reminding oneself of the value of silence and the space it offers for reflection and consideration. Over time, the deliberate practice of pausing can become a natural rhythm in conversations, a shared language of silence that enriches communication.

The power of the pause extends beyond its utility as a buffer against reactive responses or as a tool for emphasis. It serves as a testament to the complexities of human communication, a reminder that the potential for deeper understanding and connection lies in the spaces between our words. In these silences, we find room to breathe, think, and engage with each other on a level that transcends the spoken word. It's in the pause that we often see the clarity and insight that words alone cannot convey.

Thus, the pause stands not as a void but as a vessel, carrying within it the potential to deepen the connection between speaker and listener. It demands our willingness to embrace silence, not as an absence of communication but as an essential component of it. In doing so, we open ourselves to a more nuanced, thoughtful, and empathetic way of engaging with each other, where the pause becomes as powerful a tool for understanding as the words we choose to fill it with.

Question Techniques for Deeper Understanding

The dance of dialogue, intricate and revealing, finds its tempo in the questions we pose, each one an opportunity to peel back layers and explore the vast landscapes of our partner's mind and heart. The nature of our inquiries and how we frame them carry the power to open doors to uncharted territories of understanding or, conversely, to shut them, leaving mysteries untouched and potential connections unmade. The artistry lies not in asking alone but in crafting questions that invite and encourage a sharing of the self that is raw, unguarded, and profound.

Open-ended questions serve as keys to these hidden chambers, moving beyond simple yes-or-no answers to unlock the depth of thought and emotion that enrich our experiences. "What made you feel that way?" transforms a conversation from merely exchanging facts to exploring feelings, motivations, and desires. It shifts the focus from the surface to the depths, engaging our partner in a dialogue that is as much about discovery as it is about disclosure. This form of questioning does more than solicit information; it extends an invitation to wander together through the landscapes of our internal worlds, view the scenery, and share in the marvels and the mysteries within.

The delicate and deliberate phrasing of our questions can shape the terrain of the conversation, guiding it toward openness and honesty or steering it into the shadows of defensiveness and withdrawal. A question posed from a place of genuine curiosity, "Can you tell me more about what that experience was like for you?" differs vastly from one that carries the weight of judgment or accusation, "Why would you do that?" The former opens the gateway to a path leading toward understanding and empathy, while the latter erects barriers, walls that confine and divide. In the subtleties of language, we find the tools to build bridges or walls. The choice and its consequences reside in the words we select.

Approaching with sincere curiosity, free from preconceived notions or judgments, is like embarking on an uncharted journey, allowing the conversation to unfold naturally and lead wherever it may. It is an acknowledgment of our own ignorance, an admission that we do not hold all the answers, that we are here to learn, understand, and connect. This stance of openness and humility paves the way for a dialogue that is enriching for both parties, a journey of mutual discovery that strengthens the bonds of intimacy and trust.

To maneuver this terrain effectively, we arm ourselves with a repertoire of question techniques designed to delve deeper and uncover the layers beneath. These techniques, tools of the trade for any conversational explorer, include reflective questions that mirror what our partner has shared and invite them to expand upon it. "You mentioned feeling overlooked at work; what about that situation made you feel that way?" serves not only to clarify but to deepen and move closer to the core of the experience. Probing questions, however, encourages our partner to peel back their layers and explore their thoughts and feelings more thoroughly. "What do you think was driving your reaction at that moment?" prompts a self-reflection that can lead to insights and revelations, enriching the dialogue with layers of complexity and nuance.

Yet, the most potent questions are often those that remain unasked, held within the silence that punctuates our conversations. This silence, a question in itself, invites our partner to fill the space with their thoughts and feelings, to take the conversation in the direction they feel most compelled to explore. It is an offering of control, a gesture that says, "This space is yours to fill. This time is yours to shape." In this silence, we communicate our willingness to listen, to be present, and to engage with whatever our partner chooses to share. It is, perhaps, the most profound question of all, one that asks without words, "What is it that you wish to say?"

In the end, the questions we pose and how we pose them are reflections of our desire to connect, understand, and bridge the gaps that distance us from our partners. They are expressions of our curiosity, our empathy, and our commitment to our shared journey. Through our inquiries, we signal our willingness to venture into the unknown, to explore the terrains of thought and feeling that define our partner's inner world. It is in this exploration, this shared journey of discovery, that we find the essence of connection, the foundation upon which lasting relationships are built.

Feedback Loops: Constructive Conversations

In the realm of human connection, particularly within the intimate confines of a marriage, the currency of growth and understanding circulates most freely through the mechanism of feedback loops. These loops serve as conduits for exchanging perceptions and emotions, creating a dynamic environment where communication not only flows but flourishes. Within this fertile ground, conversations evolve from mere exchanges of information to rich, layered dialogues that bear the potential for profound personal and relational development.

The essence of a feedback loop in conversation lies in its capacity to foster a culture of openness and receptivity, where the sharing of thoughts and feelings is not just welcomed but actively encouraged. This encouragement stems from a mutual understanding that sharing is a gift that warrants appreciation and respect. Positive reinforcement, a critical component of this dynamic, acts as the sunlight under which the seeds of open communication germinate. A simple acknowledgment, a nod of understanding, or a word of gratitude for one's willingness to share can nourish the roots of this culture, promoting a flourishing landscape where dialogue thrives unencumbered by fear of judgment or dismissal.

Yet, cultivating constructive feedback, the very heart of effective feedback loops, requires more than just the willingness to speak and listen. It demands a level of finesse in articulating thoughts and emotions, translating internal landscapes into verbal expressions that the listener can not only hear but truly comprehend. This articulation, then, becomes a dance of sorts—a careful choreography of words and emotions that seeks to convey meaning in a manner that resonates with the listener. The dance respects the boundaries and sensitivities of the partner and navigates the delicate balance between honesty and empathy with grace and precision.

Constructive feedback, in its ideal form, moves beyond merely reporting events or behaviors to exploring the underlying emotions and needs that fuel them. It invites a deeper inquiry into the why and how, peeling back the layers to reveal the core of the issue at hand. "When you forget to call, I feel neglected" ventures further into vulnerability than a simple accusation of forgetfulness. It opens a window into the speaker's emotional world and offers the listener a glimpse of the impact of their actions, intentional or not. This approach not only fosters a deeper understanding but also paves the way for empathy and, ultimately, resolution.

Therefore, the creation of healthy feedback loops hinges on both partners' ability to direct this delicate dance of expression and reception. On one side, it calls for bravery in vulnerability, a readiness to lay bare one's thoughts and emotions in the service of mutual growth. On the other, it demands an openness of heart and mind, a willingness to receive this shared vulnerability with the respect and attentiveness it deserves. Together, these elements form the foundation of a feedback loop that enriches communication and transforms it from a mere interaction tool to a powerful engine of growth and connection.

Practical steps toward establishing these loops begin with intentionally setting space and time for open dialogue. This physical and emotional space should be one of safety and mutual respect, where distractions are minimized, and focus is placed squarely on sharing and listening. Regularly scheduled conversations focused on exploring thoughts, feelings, and needs can create a structured space where open feedback loops can thrive. Within these conversations, the practice of specific techniques, such as the use of "I" statements to express feelings and impacts, can guide the flow of communication, ensuring that it remains constructive and centered on understanding rather than blame.

Moreover, the art of giving and receiving feedback benefits from conscious practice. Engaging in reflective listening, where the listener repeats their understanding of what has been shared, offers an opportunity for clarification and deeper insight. Similarly, expressing gratitude for feedback received, regardless of its nature, reinforces the value of open communication and encourages its continuation. These practices, woven into the fabric of daily interactions, gradually shape a relationship culture where feedback loops flourish, driving growth and deepening connection.

In essence, the feedback loop stands as confirmation of the dynamic nature of communication within a marriage. It is a living, breathing process that adapts and evolves with the changing landscapes of individual and shared experiences. Through its cyclical flow of sharing, listening, and responding, it offers couples a pathway toward a deeper, more nuanced understanding of one another. It transforms conversations into opportunities for growth, healing, and reinforcement of the bonds that tether two lives together. Through consistent open dialogue, partners find clarity, resolve issues, and reaffirm their commitment to face life's complexities together, grounded in mutual understanding and respect.

TWO

Fortifying Foundations: Confronting Financial Realities Together

I n the journey of marriage, many different strands weave together to form a resilient bond. Yet, few are as delicate and potentially challenging as financial conversations. Money, with its distinct weight, often bears the paradox of being both a tool for security and a catalyst for tension. Within this delicate balance, couples find themselves charting a path lined with decisions that bear the weight of their collective future.

Navigating Financial Discussions with Ease

Money Talks: Bridging Emotional Currents with Rational Tides

Approaching financial conversations with a calm demeanor and clear mind alleviates the emotional charge often associated with money matters. Consider the scenario of planning a family vacation: budget concerns can quickly overshadow the excitement of choosing a destination. Here, open dialogue initiated in a neutral setting, perhaps a quiet evening at home after dinner, sets the stage for a constructive discussion. It's about creating an atmosphere where financial realities can be addressed without pressure, where dreams and limitations find their equilibrium in the shared vision of a memorable experience.

Crafting a Shared Financial Vision: The Blueprint of Togetherness

Setting clear financial goals is like drawing a map for a journey you plan to take together. It's not just about marking the destinations but also about charting your course to reach them. This process begins with an honest assessment of where you stand financially, individually, and as a unit. From there, it's about defining what financial success looks like for you both. Is it owning a home, saving for retirement, or ensuring a college fund for your children? Identifying these goals provides direction and fosters a sense of teamwork. It's crucial to regularly revisit these goals and make adjustments as life unfolds and priorities shift to ensure they remain aligned with your evolving aspirations.

The Pillar of Transparency: Building Trust One Disclosure at a Time

Transparency about finances is a cornerstone of trust in any relationship. It's about more than just revealing the numbers; it's about sharing aspirations, apprehensions, and everything in between. Imagine deciding to undertake a significant investment, such as purchasing a property. This venture demands not only a thorough disclosure of assets and liabilities but also an open discussion about each partner's feelings toward taking such a step—fears, expectations, and all. It's in these discussions that trust is fortified, laying a foundation solid enough to support the weight of joint financial endeavors.

Practical Steps for Harmony in Financial Dialogues

To navigate financial discussions effectively, consider these actionable steps:

1. **Schedule Financial Check-ins**: Dedicate time each month for a financial health check. This isn't merely about reviewing statements and balances but also assessing progress toward your shared goals and addressing any concerns.
2. **Create a Joint Budget**: Work together to create a budget that reflects your needs and wants. This collaborative effort ensures a realistic plan that both partners feel invested in.
3. **Agree on Your Emergency Fund**: Decide on the size and scope of an emergency fund. This mutual decision instills a sense of security, knowing you are prepared for unforeseen financial challenges.
4. **Make Investment Decisions as a Duo**: Approach investments as a team, considering each other's risk tolerance and long-term objectives. Whether it's

stocks, real estate, or retirement funds, make these decisions with a unified strategy.

5. **Be Open to Financial Counseling**: Recognize when external guidance is needed. Financial advisors or counselors can offer unbiased advice and help mediate discussions, ensuring both partners' voices are heard and respected.

Visual Element: The Financial Roadmap

A visual aid, such as a financial roadmap, can be a powerful tool for aligning financial goals and tracking progress. This roadmap might include milestones like paying off debt, savings goals, investment targets, and even dream vacations or home improvement projects. By visualizing these objectives, couples can maintain focus on their shared financial future, celebrating achievements along the way and adjusting course as necessary.

In essence, managing financial discussions with ease requires a blend of open communication, shared vision, and mutual respect. By approaching money matters as a team, couples not only build financial security but also deepen the trust and understanding that form the bedrock of their relationship. Through practical steps and ongoing dialogue, financial planning becomes a shared endeavor that strengthens the bonds of partnership.

Addressing Parenting Styles and Strategies

In marriage, maneuvering the complexities of parenting styles demands not only patience and flexibility but also an unwavering commitment to mutual respect and shared values. The divergent paths of authoritarian and permissive parenting, along with the numerous styles that fall between them, often intersect and sometimes collide within the family dynamic. At these moments, open and honest dialogue serves as the cornerstone of effective co-parenting. Through these conversations, couples can construct a unified approach, fusing individual philosophies into a cohesive strategy that honors both partners' values while prioritizing the well-being and development of their children.

Fostering Harmony Through Shared Values

At its core, the alignment of parenting strategies is less about the nuances of daily decisions and more about the underlying principles that guide those choices. It begins with exploring each partner's upbringing and the beliefs and values instilled by their parents. This reflective journey is not a quest for right or wrong but an opportunity to understand the roots of each other's parenting impulses. Through this understanding, couples can identify common ground, whether it's the importance of instilling resilience, fostering creativity, or encouraging independence. These shared values become the foundation upon which all parenting decisions are based, a touchstone that guides them through the inevitable challenges and disagreements that arise.

The Cadence of Regular Check-Ins

Regular check-ins serve as vital waypoints within the ever-evolving landscape of family life, offering opportunities to assess the terrain and adjust the course as necessary. These discussions provide a space for partners to voice concerns, celebrate successes, and recalibrate strategies in response to the changing needs of their children. They are moments for reflection, for looking beyond the immediacy of behavioral issues or academic pressures to consider the broader arc of a child's development. Within these dialogues, the focus remains firmly on the horizon—the shared vision for the kind of people they hope their children will become. It is through these regular, dedicated conversations that parenting becomes a dynamic, responsive endeavor, one that evolves in harmony with the growth of both the children and their parents.

Blending Divergent Styles: A Collection of Techniques

The combination of differing parenting styles can create a rich blend of each partner's approach rather than being a source of conflict. The key to this mixture is the mutual willingness to learn from and adapt to each other's methods. For instance, the structure and boundaries emphasized by an authoritarian approach can be softened with the empathy and flexibility characteristic of permissive parenting. Techniques for facilitating this blending process include role-playing scenarios that explore potential responses to everyday parenting challenges, from discipline to bedtime routines. These exercises illuminate the practical application of each style and foster a deeper appreciation for the merits and limitations of each approach.

Creating a parenting manual, a living document outlining agreed-upon principles and strategies, is a tangible manifestation of this blended approach. This manual, revisited and revised during regular check-ins, becomes a roadmap that offers straightforward guidance while allowing for detours as the journey develops. It's a witness to the couple's commitment to unified parenting, symbolizing their dedication to crafting a family life that reflects their individual identities and collective values.

Nurturing Unity in Diversity

Acknowledging each partner's unique contributions is paramount in the quest for a harmonized parenting approach. One may excel in nurturing creativity, and the other may bring strength in instilling discipline, but together, they create a balanced, nurturing environment. This mutual recognition not only validates each partner's role but also reinforces the notion that effective co-parenting is about complementarity, not uniformity. It's a dance of give-and-take, a delicate balance between asserting individual philosophies and embracing a unified strategy.

Ultimately, the path to effective co-parenting is both complex and rewarding, marked by continual learning, adjustment, and, above all, a deep-seated respect for each other's perspectives. When guided with care, this journey strengthens the marital bond and enriches the family dynamic. It lays the groundwork for a future where children thrive under the guidance of parents united in their love, values, and vision.

Conversations Around Intimacy and Desires

In the realm where hearts converge, and vulnerabilities are laid bare, the discourse on intimacy and desires claims its sacred ground. It demands the courage to unveil our deepest yearnings and the trust in our partner's receptiveness. Here, within the hallowed whispers of shared confidences, lies the potential to fortify the bonds of companionship or unwittingly usher in shadows of disconnect. To chart this terrain with the finesse it warrants, a meticulous approach, underscored by mutual respect and an unwavering commitment to understanding, is indispensable.

The architecture of intimacy, both physical and emotional, is inherently complex, constructed from the bricks of shared experiences, personal insecurities, and unspoken expectations. Its foundation, however, is invariably laid in the soil of communication. The cornerstone of this foundation is the ability to articulate desires and establish boundaries clearly and without fear of judgment. It transforms the act of sharing into an act of building, where each disclosed wish and acknowledged boundary adds another layer of depth to the relationship. Imagine, for a moment, the simple act of expressing a longing for more quality time together. Though seemingly straightforward, it opens the door to a more nuanced understanding of one's need for connection, offering the partner a glimpse into the emotional blueprint that guides these desires.

Yet, the path to such disclosures is often fraught with potential missteps. Misunderstandings regarding intimacy, whether borne out of unvoiced expectations or the remnants of past rejections, can erode the fabric of trust that binds. The presence of inadequacy, looming large in the wake of misconstrued desires, can silence the most earnest of conversations before they even begin. It underscores the imperative for clear, compassionate dialogue, where the focus shifts from the mere articulation of needs to an empathetic engagement with the partner's response. In this dialogue, the emphasis on mutual satisfaction becomes evident. Maintaining one's emotional integrity while tenderly handling the other's vulnerabilities is a delicate balance.

To foster such conversations, a strategic approach is advocated, one that emphasizes the gradual unveiling of desires and the thoughtful negotiation of boundaries. Initiating this dialogue in moments of tranquility, away from the immediacy of intimacy, can create a space of safety. It allows for a reflective exchange where desires and boundaries can be explored with curiosity rather than apprehension. Consider, for instance, the practice of sharing written personal reflections on intimacy penned in the quiet solitude of one's thoughts. This exchange of letters or notes can be a gentle introduction to deeper, face-to-face discussions, providing a tangible expression of one's feelings that the partner can revisit and reflect upon.

Moreover, adopting a language of affirmation alongside expressions of desire or establishing boundaries plays a pivotal role. Recognizing the importance of the relationship and the partner within it while also addressing the vulnerability of expressing unmet needs or boundaries strengthens the bond. It acts as a buffer against feelings of rejection, framing the conversation as an avenue for growth rather than a critique. The narrative thus shifts from one of deficiency to one of exploration, where the journey toward mutual fulfillment is embarked upon with enthusiasm and hope.

Interactive elements, such as guided dialogues or mutual reflection exercises, can further facilitate these conversations. These structured yet flexible tools provide a framework for discussions, ensuring that all aspects of intimacy are addressed with sensitivity and respect. They invite couples not only to articulate their desires and boundaries but also to truly listen to each other. It's in this reciprocal exchange that the essence of intimacy is distilled, revealing a connection that is continually nurtured by open, honest dialogue.

Strategies for guiding these sensitive conversations hinge not just on the willingness to share but on cultivating an environment where such sharing is received with grace and empathy. They require leaving the realm of assumption and venturing into the clarity of explicit communication. This clarity, coupled with an unwavering respect for each other's vulnerabilities, becomes the beacon that guides couples through the intricacies of intimacy and desires. It illuminates the path toward a relationship where satisfaction is not just sought but co-created, where the dance of desires and boundaries creates a bond of unparalleled depth and understanding.

Dealing with External Family Pressures

In the interconnected lives of married individuals, external pressures from family members often emerge as formidable forces capable of either fortifying or weakening the fabric of the marital bond. These pressures, subtle in their approach yet profound in their impact, necessitate a nuanced strategy that respects family ties while faithfully safeguarding the sanctity of the marital relationship. The intricate dance of balancing these external expectations with the partnership's needs and aspirations demands wisdom and a shared commitment to boundary-setting and collective decision-making. In exploring these waters, couples create a narrative that honors their union and extended family connections.

The genesis of managing family pressures lies in the recognition of their potential to strain the marital relationship. These pressures, often disguised as well-meaning advice or traditional expectations, can sneakily infiltrate the core of the partnership, planting seeds of discord and dissatisfaction. The first step, then, is to acknowledge that these influences are legitimate factors in the marital equation that deserve attention and action. This acknowledgment paves the way for open discussions where partners can voice their concerns and formulate strategies. Within this space of mutual understanding, a couple lays their foundation for managing external pressures.

Setting and enforcing boundaries with family members emerge as a critical strategy in this endeavor. Boundaries, defined not as barriers but as bridges, delineate the space where the couple's autonomy is respected, where their decisions stand firm against the tide of external opinions. This process begins with clarifying what is negotiable and untouchable within the marriage. It might involve decisions about holidays, child-rearing, or financial management, where external input often feels overwhelming. Once these boundaries are established, the next step is communication—conveying these limits to family members with firmness and compassion. This communication may be fraught with tension, but it is essential. It serves as a declaration of the couple's unity and autonomy. It says that while family ties are valued, the marital bond takes precedence.

The concept of presenting a united front in decision-making stands as a powerful tool in mitigating outside influences. This unity is not a façade; it's a manifestation of genuine consensus, a reflection of the couple's shared values and mutual respect. It requires ongoing dialogue, negotiation, and sometimes compromise, ensuring that decisions reflect the interests of the partnership above all. When faced with external pressures, a united stance sends a clear message: decisions, whether they align with familial expectations or not, are made collectively, with the relationship's well-being at heart. It transforms the couple from two individuals piloting family dynamics independently into a single, cohesive unit fortified against potential divisiveness.

Guidance on addressing and managing family pressures while maintaining healthy relationships with extended family is multifaceted. It involves a proactive approach, anticipating potential areas of conflict and discussing them before they escalate. For instance, before family gatherings, partners might discuss and agree on how to handle sensitive topics, from inquiries about starting a family to discussions about career choices or where you'll be spending the holidays. By preparing, the couple can approach such situations with confidence and cohesion and reduce the likelihood of being caught off guard by well-intentioned but intrusive questions.

Moreover, seeking external support, such as counseling or support groups, can provide couples with the tools and perspectives they need to manage family pressures effectively. These resources offer strategies for boundary-setting and communication and a space to explore the emotional impact of these pressures on the relationship. They serve as a reminder that while external family pressures are common, they are not insurmountable.

In addition, creating unique rituals and traditions can reinforce a couple's sense of us versus the world and bolster the marital bond in the face of external pressures. These rituals, whether simple nightly routines or annual vacations, become sanctuaries of connection, reminders of the shared journey, and the exclusive nature of the marital relationship. They affirm the couple's commitment to prioritizing their bond and carving out spaces of intimacy and unity amid the broader familial landscape.

In the grand scheme of things, managing external family pressures is not about building impenetrable walls but about creating a space where the bonds of family and marriage coexist in harmony. This delicate balance is achieved through open communication, mutual support, and an unwavering commitment to the partnership. Through this collaborative effort, couples can ensure that their marriage remains a haven of understanding, respect, and love, resilient in the face of external influences.

Planning for Future Goals Together

In a couple's shared life, the future often appears as a canvas awaiting the strokes of mutual aspirations and dreams. Sketching this future together, with broad sweeps and intricate details, becomes not just an exercise in goal setting but a profound affirmation of the partnership's direction and purpose. Envisioning what lies ahead offers couples a unique opportunity to blend their dreams into a unified vision that reflects the essence of their relationship.

At the heart of this endeavor lies cultivating an environment where open discussions about individual and shared aspirations can flourish. Such dialogues, rich with the potential for discovery, invite each partner to lay bare their hopes, fears, and dreams. It becomes a sacred space where the future is not imposed but imagined together, with every shared dream and every acknowledged fear drawing the partners closer. This process, however, transcends mere conversation. It involves active listening that seeks to understand not just the contours of each dream but the emotions and values that underpin them. Through this understanding, a shared vision emerges that accommodates the soaring ambitions and the quiet wishes that populate the future landscape.

Yet, the path to aligning these visions is not without its challenges. Disagreements about goals, be they related to career paths, lifestyle choices, or family planning, can test the resilience of the partnership. Here, the virtues of compromise and understanding reveal their true worth. Addressing these disagreements requires a delicate balance, a dance of give-and-take where the steps are guided by the music of mutual respect and love. It is an acknowledgment that the relationship, with its promise of a shared future, holds a value that transcends individual aspirations. Through this process, partners learn not just to negotiate their differences but to see them as opportunities for growth, as catalysts for expanding the boundaries of their shared world.

The concrete steps for setting and working toward these shared goals involve a strategic blend of planning and flexibility. Goal setting, in this context, becomes an art form where the shades of reality balance the strokes of ambition. It begins by identifying immediate and long-term objectives, each articulated with clarity and infused with the essence of the shared vision. Then comes the creation of a roadmap, a detailed plan that outlines the steps required to transform these objectives into reality. This roadmap, however, is not set in stone. It is a living document responsive to the inevitable shifts in circumstances and aspirations that accompany the passage of time. Regular reviews and adjustments ensure that the roadmap remains aligned with the evolving contours of the relationship and the external world.

In instances where visions for the future diverge, the reconciliation of these differences becomes a testament to the strength of the partnership. This reconciliation is rooted in the recognition that the essence of compromise lies not in the diminishment of individual dreams but in creating a shared reality that honors the spirit of those dreams. It involves a deep dive into the underlying values that drive these aspirations and a search for common ground that can serve as the foundation for a future that reflects the best of both partners. The process is underscored by an unwavering commitment to the relationship, a recognition that the journey together is as important as the destination.

Strategies for moving through this terrain vary significantly. Some couples may choose to create a vision board, a visual representation of their goals that serves as a powerful tool for maintaining focus and fostering motivation. Others might adopt a more analytical approach, setting milestones and establishing regular check-ins to monitor progress. Regardless of the method, the underlying principle remains the same: planning for the future is an ongoing dialogue, a continuous negotiation between the individual's dreams and the partnership's aspirations.

As this chapter draws to a close, we are reminded of the transformative power of planning for future goals together. This process, with its blend of open dialogue, mutual understanding, and strategic action, not only fortifies the bond between partners but also illuminates the path ahead with the light of shared purpose. It reaffirms the notion that a relationship, at its best, is a partnership not just in the trials of the present but in the dreams of the future. As we move forward, the journey continues, with each step guided by the shared vision that emerges from the hearts and minds of those who walk together.

THREE

The Pillars of Trust: Everyday Acts That Fortify Bonds

I n relationships, trust is not a single entity but a collection of countless small actions and words. Over time, these pieces come together to create a picture of reliability and safety. It's not merely grand gestures but a multitude of small, seemingly inconsequential acts that layer one upon another to construct the basis of trust. This understanding shifts the focus from seeking monumental proofs of loyalty to recognizing the power of the everyday moments that, when combined, build a foundation of trust that is both resilient and nurturing.

Daily Trust-Building Activities

The Subtle Blend of Kindness and Reliability

At first glance, an act of kindness—a note tucked into a lunch bag, a cup of coffee brought unasked—may appear to be a simple gesture of affection. Yet, beneath its surface, such actions are threads in the fabric of trust, each one evidence of attentiveness and care. They say, quietly but unmistakably, "You are seen; you are valued." Similarly, reliability, the act of following through on promises and commitments, however small, speaks volumes. It transforms words into truths and promises into certainties. A partner who takes out the trash every Tuesday evening, rain or shine, and without fail, is not just performing a household task but is also enacting a ritual of reliability. Over time, these actions accumulate, each a brick in building trust.

Consistency: The Heartbeat of Trust

The rhythm of trust is marked by consistency, a steady pulse of dependable actions and behaviors that, like a heartbeat, signal health and vitality in the relationship. It's found in the daily rituals—the routines that, while mundane, create a pattern of predictability and security. Consider the ritual nightly phone call when one partner is away on business. This consistent connection, this end-of-day check-in, becomes more than a conversation; it becomes a lifeline, a tangible reminder that, despite the distance, the bond remains intact.

Practical Trust-Building Activities

To cultivate trust through daily actions, consider incorporating specific, intentional activities into your routine. These need not be elaborate; their power lies in their regularity and the sincerity behind them.

- **Morning Affirmations**: Start each day with a positive affirmation, a simple statement of appreciation or support for your partner. This sets a tone of positivity and connection for the day ahead.
- **The Trust Jar**: Create a physical manifestation of trust by filling a jar with notes, each detailing an act of faith or kindness you've observed in your partner. Gradually filled, this visual representation becomes a powerful symbol of the trust built over time.
- **Shared Goals Checklist**: Together, compile a list of small, achievable goals, whether related to household tasks, personal projects, or relationship milestones. Review and check off the completed items regularly to reinforce teamwork and reliability.

Visual Element: The Trust Mosaic

Consider creating a trust map, a visual representation of the daily acts of kindness and reliability that form the foundation of trust. This can take the form of a poster or a digital collage, with each piece representing an action or gesture that has bolstered trust within the relationship. This map, evolving over time, serves as a poignant reminder that everyday moments have the power to create a resilient and loving partnership.

In sum, building trust is an exercise in patience and attentiveness, a daily practice of kindness, reliability, and consistency. It recognizes that trust is not a given but a gift, one that is continually crafted and nurtured through the smallest of actions. Through intentional practices and the creation of symbolic representations such as the trust map, couples can deepen their understanding of trust and fortify the bonds that unite them.

The Role of Vulnerability in Trust

In the heart of marriage, vulnerability, while delicate, holds immense potential for strength. This paradox, where opening oneself to potential hurt becomes a conduit for deeper connection, underscores vulnerability as a pivotal element in the framework of trust. It is within the act of baring one's soul—revealing fears, desires, and the soft underbelly of personal struggles—that the true essence of trust is tested and fortified. Far from being a sign of weakness, vulnerability emerges as a fortress of strength, a testimony to the belief in the other's capacity for empathy and understanding.

Revealing one's innermost self to another is complex, especially in a lifelong partnership. It involves a deliberate unmasking, a choice to stand unguarded in the light of the other's gaze. This act is inherently fraught with risk; it requires a foundational belief in the partner's kindness and faith that the exposed heart will be met not with judgment but with acceptance. When this faith is rewarded, the roots of trust delve deeper and anchor the relationship against the uproars of doubt and insecurity. It is in these moments of mutual vulnerability, when fears and desires are shared without pretense, that the bond between partners transcends the superficial and creates a connection rich with intimacy and authenticity.

However, the path to fostering an environment where vulnerability can flourish is not without obstacles. The shadows of past hurts, the echoes of rejection, can cast long shadows, chilling the willingness to open up. Overcoming these barriers requires not only individual courage but also a concerted effort to create a safe space where vulnerabilities can be expressed without fear. This begins with an explicit agreement to honor each other's courage and to treat shared secrets and fears with the reverence they deserve. Such an agreement, spoken or unspoken, becomes the scaffold upon which trust is built, a mutual understanding that the shared vulnerability is sacred, a no-man's-land where judgment is banished, and empathy reigns supreme.

There are numerous strategies for exploring the vulnerable terrain of each other's inner world, yet all are rooted in the principles of safety, respect, and unconditional acceptance. Initiating conversations about fears and desires might start in the shallow end, sharing small insecurities or minor concerns as a way to test the waters. These initial outings into vulnerability are crucial; they set a precedent, establishing patterns of reaction and support that pave the way for deeper disclosures. As trust deepens, so does the capacity for sharing the more profound and often more painful truths of one's experience.

Creating rituals around these disclosures can give them both gravity and comfort. A regular, perhaps weekly, "Heart Talk" —a dedicated time for open, vulnerable conversation—can provide a consistent outlet for this level of sharing. This ritual, marked by a physical setting that encourages intimacy (e.g., a quiet room, soft lighting, perhaps an agreement to hold hands), signals that this is a time apart from the ordinary, a space where the standard rules of engagement are suspended in favor of raw honesty.

In these dialogues, the art of listening becomes as important as the act of sharing. Authentic listening in this context is active, an engagement that involves not just the ears but the heart. It's about hearing not only words but the emotions, unspoken fears, and unvoiced dreams behind them. This kind of listening fosters empathy, allowing the listener to inhabit, as much as one person can, the emotional landscape of their partner. It transforms vulnerability from a one-sided exposition to a shared journey, a mutual exploration of the depths of each other's being.

Moreover, reflecting on what one hears validates the sharer's openness and reinforces the vulnerability's safety. This reflection is not parroting; it's empathetic mirroring that says, "I see you; I hear you, and what you've shared matters deeply to me." It's a form of feedback that, in its acknowledgment and acceptance, becomes a powerful tool for deepening trust.

Yet, the most potent strategy for encouraging vulnerability may lie in the willingness to go first. By taking the initial step into the arena of openness and by being the first to share fears, desires, or insecurities, one partner can lead by example. This act of bravery, of vulnerability without guarantee of reciprocation, is a beacon. It lights the way for the other, offering both a model of courage and an implicit promise of a safe landing. It says, without words, "This is a space where we can be our truest selves together."

In essence, the interplay of vulnerability and trust within the confines of a marriage is a dance of light and shadow, of risk and reward. It is a process that, while fraught with potential for pain, holds within it the promise of unparalleled depth of connection. By intentionally sharing, listening, and validating each other and having the courage to be the first to open, couples can successfully manage the complexities of their relationship. They can turn vulnerability from a source of fear into a source of strength, creating a continuous flow of trust that revitalizes and enriches their shared life.

Rebuilding Trust After a Breach

In the intricate dynamics of a relationship, the bond of trust, once damaged, demands both the willingness to repair and the skilled hands of both partners to mend. After being mended, the connection bears the marks of its restoration, serving as a reflection of resilience and the labor of love. The breach of trust, whether through deceit, betrayal, or broken promises, creates a crack that disrupts the previously smooth surface of connection. Yet, while painful, this disruption is not a foregone conclusion to an end but rather a difficult passage that, approached with care, can lead to a stronger connection.

The cornerstone of this delicate repair work lies in the authenticity of apologies. To go beyond just words and truly reach the heart of the pain, an apology must carry the weight of genuine remorse. It is an acknowledgment of the pain caused, an understanding of the depth of the breach, and a commitment to change. But this commitment is rendered hollow without actions to manifest it. In this context, change is not a sole adjustment of behaviors but a deeper transformation in attitudes, a shift in the very system that led to the breach. The promise not to repeat the hurtful action is intertwined with the effort to understand its origins and to actively work on the underlying issues, whether related to communication, boundaries, or unmet needs.

This inherently slow process is a test of patience for both parties. The one who has been wronged grapples with the shadows of hurt, the wavering between the pain of the past and the hope for the future. Patience, then, is not a passive waiting but an active engagement in healing, a choice to stay in the space of discomfort with the hope of emerging into a place of understanding and forgiveness. Forgiveness, in turn, is not a deletion of memory but a decision not to let that memory dictate the future. It is a gift, not just to the one who caused the hurt but to oneself, a release from the chain of resentment that binds the heart to pain. This release, however, does not preclude the necessity for accountability. The one who broke the trust must be willing to live under the microscope of scrutiny to have their actions and intentions examined as they work to rebuild the trust they've lost.

The roadmap to restoring trust is paved with transparency and reliability. Transparency acts as a clear window through which the actions of the one who broke trust can be seen, unclouded by doubts or secrets. It involves an openness about one's movements, decisions, and interactions, inviting the other to witness one's commitment to change. Reliability, the consistent demonstration of changed behavior, reinforces this transparency. It is through consistent actions over time, honoring promises made and commitments kept, that the fragile beginnings of trust begin to take root again.

This journey of repair is marked by milestones, each one a step toward the re-establishment of trust. The first is the acknowledgment of the hurt caused, followed closely by the sincere apology and the expressed commitment to change. The subsequent milestones are less about declarations and more about deeds, the visible efforts to address the issues that led to the breach. These efforts might encompass seeking professional help, attending therapy, or engaging in relationship workshops, all aimed at acquiring the tools to guide the relationship with greater care and understanding.

An essential part of this process is the creation of a new narrative for the relationship, one that acknowledges the breach but does not allow it to define the entirety of the connection. This narrative, co-authored by both partners, weaves in the lessons learned from the breach, the insights gained through the process of repair, and the vision for the future. It reframes the breach not as the end but as a pivot, a point around which the relationship evolves into something more resilient, more aware of its vulnerabilities, and more committed to safeguarding the trust that forms its core.

As this chapter on rebuilding trust unfolds, devoid of a neat closure or a grand summary, it mirrors the reality of trust repair in the realm of relationships. It is a process without a definitive end, a journey marked by progress and setbacks, hope and doubt. Yet, in the willingness to engage in this labor of love and the commitment to reconnecting the bonds of trust, couples find not just the path back to each other but also a deeper, more authentic connection.

Setting Boundaries to Protect Trust

In the heart of every flourishing relationship, boundaries stand as silent sentinels, safeguarding the sanctity of trust and mutual respect. These invisible lines, drawn not in sand but in the firmer soil of understanding and agreement, define what is permissible and what is not. They act as a guide, outlining the relationship's landscape and ensuring both individuals move through this shared space without unintentionally entering areas of discomfort or disrespect. In setting boundaries, partners engage in a dialogue that is as much about protecting the individual self as it is about nurturing the collective bond, a delicate balance between autonomy and intimacy.

Boundaries, in their essence, are declarations of self-respect and respect for the other, a mutual acknowledgment of each partner's inherent worth and autonomy. They emerge from a place of self-awareness, a deep understanding of one's needs, limits, and expectations. When shared openly and received with empathy, this awareness becomes the foundation upon which trust is built and maintained. It is a process that transforms vulnerability into strength, where revealing one's boundaries becomes an act of trust. In sharing what we hold most private, we place our faith in our partner's capacity to honor and uphold these boundaries, just as they trust us to do the same.

The negotiation of boundaries is a back-and-forth dance that requires not just listening but truly hearing, not just speaking but communicating. It is an exercise in precision, as the language used to articulate boundaries must be clear and straightforward, free from the shadows of implication or assumption. This clarity ensures that there is no room for misunderstanding and no space for the unintended crossing of lines that could lead to hurt or betrayal. It requires a level of honesty that, while challenging, deepens the connection between partners and reinforces the trust that each will act with consideration and care.

In discussing and setting these boundaries, partners engage in an act of co-creation, a joint effort to sculpt the contours of their relationship in a way that respects and reflects the needs of both individuals. This process, far from being a one-time conversation, is ongoing, a dialogue that evolves as the relationship grows and changes. It acknowledges that we are not static; our needs, like our boundaries, may shift over time. Regular check-ins, moments set aside to revisit and, if necessary, renegotiate these boundaries, ensure that they remain relevant and respected, a true reflection of the current state of the relationship.

Practical tips for setting and communicating healthy boundaries begin with recognizing the need for such boundaries. This recognition often arises from moments of discomfort or conflict that signal something out of alignment within the relationship. It calls for introspection, a period of reflection to identify the root of this discomfort and the boundaries that can alleviate it. Once identified, the next step is to communicate these boundaries to one's partner in an assertive and compassionate manner. This communication is not about laying down ultimatums but about opening a dialogue, an invitation to understand and be understood.

Examples of boundaries that protect trust might include agreements about time spent with friends or how financial resources are allocated. They might encompass expectations around communication, such as how disagreements are handled or how much personal information is shared with others outside the relationship. While varied in scope, these boundaries share a common purpose: to create a framework within which the relationship can thrive, free from the resentment or misunderstanding that can erode trust.

In setting and communicating boundaries, the language used is pivotal. It should be direct yet free from aggression, firm yet infused with kindness. Phrases like "I feel" or "I need" place the focus on the individual's experience, reducing the likelihood of defensive reactions. They invite a response rather than demand compliance, fostering a spirit of cooperation. This cooperative spirit is further nurtured by the willingness to listen to and respect the boundaries set by one's partner. This give-and-take is the hallmark of a healthy relationship.

In the end, boundaries are not barriers but bridges, structures that define the space between individuals and serve to connect them more deeply. They are an affirmation of each partner's individuality within the unity of the relationship, a declaration that while we are together, we are also ourselves. This delicate balance, maintained through the setting and respecting of boundaries, becomes the soil in which trust grows. This trust is robust, resilient, and able to withstand the challenges that relationships inevitably face. In this space, safeguarded by boundaries, trust flourishes, nurtured by the understanding, respect, and care each partner extends to the other.

Trust and Technology: Navigating the Digital Age

In modern relationships, technology significantly impacts the foundational trust, shaping the strength and dynamics of the bond. The digital age, with its countless connections, has introduced both tools for building bridges and the potential for creating divides between partners. The key lies not in the technology itself but in how couples direct its use, striking a balance that fosters trust without encroaching on the sanctity of individual autonomy.

Digital communication has reshaped the landscape of trust, presenting scenarios unimagined in previous generations. Text messages, social media, and emails offer platforms for connection, yet they also open avenues for misunderstandings and misgivings. The immediacy and permanence of digital interactions necessitate a nuanced approach to trust—one that accommodates these new ways of connecting while safeguarding the core values of honesty and transparency. To maneuver this terrain, open discussions about digital boundaries emerge as pivotal. Though potentially fraught with sensitivities, these dialogues are essential in delineating what each partner deems respectful and acceptable within the digital domain. They cover the spectrum of online behaviors, from sharing personal information to interactions with others on social media platforms. Without these discussions, assumptions flourish, breeding grounds for doubts and insecurities that can erode the foundations of trust.

In the delicate balance between transparency and privacy, password sharing often surfaces as a benchmark test for trust. On one hand, shared passwords can symbolize an open book policy, a gesture of unrestricted trust and willingness to share one's digital world with the other. On the other hand, the expectation of such sharing can be perceived as a breach of personal autonomy, a sign of mistrust that undermines the individual's right to privacy. The resolution to this problem does not lie in a universal prescription but in the mutual understanding reached by each couple. It requires a dialogue that respects both the desire for openness and the need for personal space, acknowledging that trust is not measured by accessibility to one's private messages but by the integrity of one's actions both online and offline.

Guidance on balancing technology use with trust-building is multifaceted, acknowledging the complexity of digital interactions. Setting digital boundaries is a collaborative process involving both partners in a dialogue about their expectations, fears, and desires regarding technology use. This conversation might cover topics as varied as the appropriateness of online friendships, sharing photos on social media, or the boundaries around work-related communications outside of office hours. The aim is to establish a set of guidelines that both partners feel comfortable with, rules that respect each individual's privacy while ensuring that the digital world becomes a space of connection rather than contention.

This guidance involves practical steps to direct technology in ways that enhance rather than detract from the relationship. It might involve agreed-upon 'tech-free' times when devices are set aside to prioritize face-to-face interactions. Similarly, decisions about online activities, from the content shared on social media to the people with whom each partner interacts, can be made with consideration for the other's feelings and comfort levels. By actively choosing to engage with technology in ways that reflect mutual respect and understanding, couples reinforce the trust that forms the bedrock of their relationship.

In the final analysis, the role of technology in modern relationships is comparable to that of any tool; its value is determined by the hands that wield it. When used with intention and care, it has the potential to build bridges of understanding and connection. Yet, without the guiding principles of honesty, transparency, and mutual respect, it can drive partners apart. The journey through the digital age is one that couples must maneuver together, armed with open dialogue, agreed-upon boundaries, and a commitment to use technology to strengthen the fabric of their relationship.

As we close this exploration of trust in the digital age, the overarching themes of communication, transparency, and mutual respect echo as enduring principles. They remind us that, amid the rapid advancements of technology, the timeless values of trust remain unchanged. In the next chapter, this foundation sets the stage for delving deeper into the intricacies of intimacy, exploring how the bridges of trust we build serve as the pathways to deeper, more meaningful connections.

FOUR

Innovating Intimacy: Breathing New Life into Date Nights

Date nights, the classic emblem of romantic endeavor, often fall prey to the comfort of routine, morphing into a predictable scenario of dinner and a movie. Yet, the essence of a truly enriching date night lies not in the activity itself but in its capacity to foster connection, to serve as a bridge over the mundane toward a place of shared discovery and joy. The evolution of this cherished tradition into something that surprises and delights requires a departure from the familiar, an exploration of the path less traveled that leads couples to new experiences and, ultimately, a deeper bond.

Reimagining Date Night: Ideas Beyond Dinner and a Movie

Breaking the Mold: Venturing into Uncharted Waters

The novel's appeal lies not just in the experience but in the anticipation it stirs, a spark that ignites the imagination and awakens a sense of adventure. Consider the planning of a surprise date night, where one partner curates an evening based on a shared yet unexplored interest—perhaps a night at an observatory for a couple fascinated by the cosmos or a cooking class featuring flavors they've yet to taste. This endeavor, cloaked in secrecy, adds layers to the excitement as each partner engages in a silent dance of hints and guesses, the anticipation building to a crescendo until the moment of revelation.

The Symphony of Shared Activities

The power of shared activities to fortify bonds lies in their ability to act as conduits for mutual growth and discovery. Engaging in an activity that neither partner has tried before, whether salsa dancing under the stars or kayaking through peaceful waters at dawn, serves as a canvas for creating new memories, a mutual venture into the unknown that fosters reliance and teamwork. It's in these moments, away from the comfort of familiar settings, that partners find new facets of each other, and each discovery deepens their relationship, helping to build a stronger and more meaningful connection.

The Art of Planning and Anticipation

When approached collaboratively, planning a date night transforms from a task into an adventure. Setting aside time to brainstorm ideas, perhaps through a shared digital document to which both partners can contribute thoughts and inspiration, turns planning into a joint venture. Engaging both partners in the creation of the evening ensures that the final plan resonates with mutual desires and makes antici-pating the event a shared experience that starts long before the date itself.

Reflective Discussions Post-Date

The conclusion of a date night marks the beginning of another integral phase—the reflective discussion. Engaging in a conversation about the evening's experiences and sharing what each found surprising, delightful, or even challenging deepens the emotional connection. This exchange, perhaps over a cup of coffee the following morning, allows partners to express appreciation for the effort and thought invested in the date and to voice desires and ideas for future adventures. It is in these discussions that the essence of the date night is distilled, and its impact on the relationship is understood and appreciated.

Visual Element: The Date Night Jar

A physical element that can enhance the anticipation and planning of date nights is the creation of a Date Night Jar. Couples can fill a decorative jar with written ideas for future dates, with each suggestion written on a colorful piece of paper. This jar, placed in a prominent location, serves as a visual reminder of the adventures that await, a reservoir of inspiration that can be drawn upon whenever the routine threatens to take hold. On a chosen day, one partner can select a note at random and set the stage for the next shared adventure. This simple yet interactive element not only aids in the planning process but also injects an element of spontaneity and excitement into the anticipation of date night.

In reimagining date night, couples embark on a journey that transcends the simplicity of shared activities to touch the core of what it means to grow together. It is a testament to the belief that the pursuit of novelty and the courage to step beyond the familiar can breathe new life into a couple's connection. Through innovative ideas, collaborative planning, and reflective conversations, date night becomes more than an event—it becomes a doorway to deeper intimacy and a more vibrant partnership.

The Intimacy Inventory: Assessing and Growing Your Connection

The cultivation of intimacy, an endeavor as delicate as it is profound, demands not only the willingness to explore the depths of one's relationship but also the tools to manage this exploration. Enter the concept of the Intimacy Inventory, a methodical approach designed to map the contours of a couple's emotional landscape. This tool, both mirror and map, reflects the current state of the connection while charting a course for its enrichment. In its essence, the Intimacy Inventory acts as a beacon that guides partners through the sometimes murky waters of emotional connectivity to shores of deeper understanding and closeness.

Building this inventory begins with assembling questions that probe the breadth and depth of the partnership's emotional and physical connection. These inquiries range from exploring shared dreams and fears to evaluating communication patterns and expressions of affection. The aim here is not merely to catalog aspects of the relationship but to unearth the underlying dynamics that shape them. Questions like "In what moments do you feel most connected to me?" or "What words or actions do you find most affirming of our bond?" serve as keys, unlocking insights into the nuanced interplay of needs, desires, and expressions of love within the partnership.

In the application of the Intimacy Inventory, timing and setting play pivotal roles. A quiet, undisturbed space, free from the distractions of daily life, sets the stage for this introspective journey. Approached with open hearts and minds, the inventory becomes a ritual of connection, an opportunity for partners not only to share but to truly hear and see each other anew. As each question unfolds, layers of understanding are added, revealing not only areas of strength but also those in need of tender care and attention.

Addressing gaps in intimacy, as illuminated by the inventory's outcomes, requires a nuanced approach, one that balances sensitivity with a proactive stance. Strategies for bridging these gaps may involve the initiation of new rituals of connection, such as dedicated time for conversation, shared hobbies, or practices designed to enhance physical closeness. The key lies in acknowledging that these gaps are not failures but opportunities for growth, signposts guiding the relationship toward greater depth and fulfillment. For instance, if the inventory reveals a longing for more quality time together, partners might create a weekly 'us' night dedicated solely to nurturing their bond away from the routines of work and family obligations.

Conversely, the inventory also illuminates areas where the connection thrives, where intimacy blossoms in full strength. Recognizing and celebrating these strengths is as crucial as identifying the gaps. It affirms the love and effort that sustain the relationship, serving as a source of confidence and joy for both partners. Celebrations of these strengths might manifest in simple acknowledgments and expressions of gratitude for the ways each partner contributes to the flourishing of their bond. Or, they might take the form of shared experiences, special dates, or activities planned around these areas of strong connection, reinforcing the behaviors and patterns that nurture intimacy.

In its entirety, the Intimacy Inventory highlights the evolving nature of relationships. It reminds us that intimacy, in all its forms, requires not just the initial spark of connection but the ongoing kindling of attention, understanding, and care. By regularly engaging with this tool, couples ensure that the evolution of their bond is marked not by the accumulation of unspoken needs and missed connections but by a deepening closeness that stands the test of time.

Physical Touch Beyond Sex: The Language of Non-Sexual Affection

In the elaborate exchange of closeness that characterizes the bonds of intimacy within a partnership, the subtle gestures of non-sexual touch often speak volumes, articulating sentiments that words may struggle to convey. This form of communication, relying on the warmth of a gentle touch or the security of a firm grasp, operates on a primal level, evoking a sense of belonging and mutual respect that is foundational to the development of a deeper, more nuanced connection. It is within these silent exchanges that the essence of love and care is often most noticeably felt, serving as a reminder of the physical presence and emotional support that partners offer one another.

The spectrum of non-sexual touch encompasses a wide array of gestures, each bearing a unique signature and significance. A gentle touch exchanged amidst laughter, fingers entwined as a movie unfolds on the screen, or the comforting embrace that follows a day fraught with challenges—these seemingly mundane actions carry deep significance. They serve as tangible manifestations of affection, reinforcing the bond that exists beyond sexual intimacy. This physical contact acts as a bridge that closes the distance that daily routines and external pressures may impose. It ensures that physical and emotional closeness remains a constant, nurturing presence in the relationship.

Incorporating daily rituals of non-sexual touching into the fabric of a partnership offers a steady stream of connection, a rhythmic reminder of the love and care that binds. Establishing these rituals can be as simple as a hug before the day begins. This brief gesture embodies a wealth of affection and support. Similarly, a nightly foot rub, offered without the expectation of reciprocation, becomes a soothing balm, easing the stresses of the day while affirming the commitment to nurture and cherish. Woven into the routine of life, these daily practices become markers of stability and safety, islands of tranquility in the frequently chaotic sea of daily existence.

Yet, the path to integrating non-sexual touch into the rhythm of a relationship is not without its hurdles. Barriers to physical closeness, whether rooted in past experiences, present insecurities, or simply the ups and downs of life's responsibilities, can dampen the willingness to reach out or to receive. Overcoming these barriers requires not only a conscious effort but also a compassionate understanding of the underlying causes. It calls for open dialogues where fears and hesitations can be shared without the fear of judgment and where the desire for closeness is not overshadowed by the vulnerability of exposure. Through these conversations, a mutual understanding emerges, one that respects individual comfort levels while gently nudging the boundaries, encouraging a gradual opening to the possibilities that non-sexual touch offers.

The cultivation of an environment conducive to the free exchange of affectionate touches hinges on the recognition of touch as a language in its own right, one that communicates love, reassurance, and connection. It necessitates an attunement to the partner's cues, a sensitivity to the moments when a touch can be soothing, and those when space is needed. This attunement, fostered through attentive observation and empathetic engagement, ensures that the gestures of affection resonate with the intended warmth and care, reinforcing the bond rather than inadvertently straining it.

In essence, the realm of non-sexual touch provides a wealth of opportunities for partners to express their affection and solidify their bond through the simple act of reaching out. It highlights the power of physical closeness to elevate everyday experiences and transform everyday moments into opportunities for connection and intimacy. Through the conscious incorporation of these gestures into the daily life of a partnership, couples can address the complexities of their relationship with a renewed sense of closeness and understanding, fortified by the silent language of non-sexual affection.

Emotional Intimacy Exercises: Deepening Your Emotional Bond

The foundation of a strong relationship is built not only on shared joys but also on the deep connections formed in moments of emotional intimacy. This profound layer, where souls converse without words, demands more than passive coexistence; it calls for deliberate actions, for exercises that bridge distances unseen and knit hearts closer with every shared secret and every disclosed fear. Within this sacred space, emotional intimacy becomes the cornerstone upon which the edifice of a relationship rests, a beacon that illuminates the path to a bond that is unshakable and profound.

To nurture this emotional intimacy, specific exercises emerge as tools, each designed to peel back layers to reveal the core where true connection resides. Shared journaling, an endeavor both simple and profound, offers a window into the heart's inner workings. Here, within the pages of a shared diary, partners articulate thoughts unspoken, dreams unshared, and fears that lurk in silence. This act of writing becomes a dialogue, a call and response where each entry, a reflection of words, reveals the soul. Partners take turns writing, reading, and then writing again, a cycle that transforms individual musings into a shared narrative. In this narrative, vulnerability finds its strength; the courage to be open, to be seen in one's entirety, becomes the thread that binds more tightly than any vow.

Storytelling, another vessel for deepening emotional understanding, pulls from the well of past experiences and draws forth memories that are shaped, molded, and defined. Seated together, perhaps under a canopy of stars or in the warmth of a shared blanket, partners take turns unveiling stories of their past, tales of triumphs and tribulations. This exchange, more than mere recollection, invites a partner into the sacred space of personal history, sharing the experiences and memories that, when combined, create a complete picture of who they are. It is an exercise in listening, not only to the words spoken but to the emotional echoes behind them, fostering empathy that deepens the bond and creates a shared history from their individual pasts.

Embracing vulnerability within these exercises serves not as an act of surrender but as a declaration of strength, a reflection of the trust that forms the foundation of the partnership. To lay bare one's fears and desires demands faith in the other's capacity for kindness, an unspoken pact that this openness will be met with warmth and acceptance. This vulnerability, far from a weakness, becomes the crucible in which the relationship is refined, only to emerge stronger and more resilient. It is in these moments, when defenses fall away, and hearts lay exposed, that emotional intimacy blossoms, unfurling like a flower to the sun, its petals the moments of shared vulnerability that color the relationship.

Regular emotional check-ins anchor this practice of deepening emotional intimacy. As islands of tranquility in the commotion of daily life, they provide a structured space for partners to voice their emotional needs and disclose their concerns. Here, within the safety of a designated time and space, emotions and needs articulate themselves free from the distortions of stress or distraction. These discussions, while at times challenging, serve as the basis that supports the relationship, where each action represents a concern addressed, a need fulfilled, and a bond strengthened. They demand honesty and an openness to speak and hear truths that are uncomfortable yet necessary. In this honesty, trust deepens, for it is built not on the absence of conflict but on the ability to manage the emotional complexities with empathy and understanding.

The culmination of these exercises transforms the relationship, fortifying its foundations through the deliberate practice of building emotional intimacy. Shared journaling and storytelling become sacred acts that celebrate the depth of the bond. Vulnerability, once a shadowed path, now shines as a beacon, guiding the relationship toward an unimagined closeness. Regular emotional check-ins stand as milestones, markers of progress on the journey toward a partnership defined by its depth of understanding and emotional connection.

In this environment, where emotional intimacy flourishes through the efforts of both partners, the relationship finds its strength. It demonstrates the power of deliberate action and exercises designed not just to maintain but to deepen the emotional bond. Here, in the shared spaces of vulnerability and understanding, love finds its fullest expression, and the partnership finds its most profound fulfillment.

Technology for Two: Apps and Digital Tools to Enhance Intimacy

As the digital world merges with daily life, the relationship between technology and intimacy emerges, revealing a range of possibilities where bytes and pixels serve not as barriers but as bridges to deeper connections. The thoughtful integration of apps and digital tools into the realm of romantic partnerships offers avenues to enhance the bond that connects hearts through a collection of shared experiences, growth, and communication.

At the forefront of this exploration stands a curated selection of digital offerings designed to fortify the bonds of affection between partners. Among these, apps that facilitate the sharing of thoughts and schedules allow couples to remain linked in each other's lives, regardless of physical distance. Tools such as shared calendars and to-do lists provide a canvas for collaboration, turning mundane tasks into opportunities for connection. Meanwhile, platforms dedicated to the expression of gratitude and affection offer a space where the currency of love is exchanged through words and images, where each entry is a digital love letter that testifies to the enduring presence of affection.

Yet, the world of apps extends beyond the logistical, venturing into territories ripe with potential for growth. Applications that prompt daily questions encourage partners to delve into discussions that might otherwise remain unexplored, with each query laying a stepping stone toward deeper understanding. Similarly, platforms that offer guided relationship exercises transform the screen into a space of mutual discovery where challenges are encountered and overcome together, and each victory serves as a building block that strengthens the bond.

As we engage in this digital environment, establishing boundaries becomes essential, serving as a guide to ensure that technology enhances our connections rather than distances us. This negotiation of digital boundaries demands a dialogue marked by honesty and openness, one that honors each individual's comfort with online sharing and communication. It is a delicate balance of respect for personal digital spaces and the desire for transparency, and each decision reflects mutual values and trust.

The creative application of technology in maintaining and enhancing intimacy breathes life into the connection, offering new dimensions to the experience of togetherness. Shared playlists of songs that resonate with moments of joy, struggle, and triumph become soundtracks of the relationship; each note a memory, and each melody a shared emotion. Video diary exchanges offer windows into each other's worlds, capturing moments of solitude and reflection and creating a portrait of the individual within the collective journey of the partnership.

In exploring technology's role in intimacy, a dynamic process emerges, shaped by how digital interactions enhance or challenge emotional connection, shared experiences, or the boundaries that define them. It is a landscape where technology acts as a weld, uniting partners in a dance of growth, understanding, and affection. Through the thoughtful selection and use of apps and tools, couples progress through the waters of their relationship with a renewed sense of connection, each digital interaction a step toward a deeper bond.

As this chapter draws to a close, integrating technology into romantic partnerships isn't just a challenge but an opportunity where digital connections blend with emotions, transforming bytes and pixels into tools for strengthening bonds and shared dreams. The curated selection of apps and tools, the thoughtful negotiation of digital boundaries, and the creative employment of technology emerge as pillars upon which the modern relationship stands, fortified against the pressures of distance and time. In this world, technology serves as a symbol of the enduring power of love, a reminder that in the hands of those committed to the journey of togetherness, even the digital can become personal, intimate, and profoundly human.

As we transition from the digital environment that shapes the contours of modern intimacy, our gaze shifts toward the horizon of commitment, where the vows of partnership are tested and tempered. The journey continues, each step reflecting the resilience, growth, and enduring affection that defines the shared path of love.

FIVE

Transforming Conflict into Connection

J ust as an untended garden sprouts weeds that threaten the vitality of its flowers, unresolved conflicts in a marriage can overshadow the beauty of the bond. Like the skilled gardener who identifies and addresses the root cause of the infestation, couples must dig beneath the surface of their disputes to unearth the underlying issues. Within this excavation lies the potential not just for resolution but for growth, turning battlegrounds into fertile ground for understanding and closeness.

Identifying the Root Causes of Conflicts

At the heart of most conflicts lies a tangled web of unmet needs, unspoken assumptions, and unresolved issues. The task of unraveling this web begins with the recognition that the topics of disagreements often serve as mere proxies for deeper and more complex emotional undercurrents. Reflective listening and asking open-ended questions illuminate the hidden layers beneath the surface, revealing the true nature of the conflict. They are as indispensable to this task as sunlight and water are to a garden's growth.

Techniques That Uncover What Lies Beneath

Imagine a scenario where a couple finds themselves at odds over how to spend their weekends. On the surface, it appears to be a simple clash of preferences—outdoor activities versus quiet time at home. But through reflective listening, one partner might discover that the other's insistence on spending weekends outdoors stems from a deeper need for adventure and novelty, a need that traces back to a youth spent in a stifling, restrictive environment. This revelation shifts the conversation from one of contention to one of understanding and empathy.

Recognizing Patterns in Conflicts

Conflicts often reveal underlying issues or unmet needs, serving as important indicators of what might be unresolved. A couple may notice that their disagreements intensify during periods of stress or transition, suggesting that the root cause may not be the topics of the disputes themselves but an underlying feeling of insecurity or lack of support. By mapping these patterns and addressing the foundational issues before they surface, couples can begin to anticipate and mitigate conflicts.

Strategies for Addressing Core Issues

The process of addressing these core issues requires a willingness to engage in difficult conversations and peel back the layers of the self and the relationship. It involves setting aside time and space for these discussions and approaching them with an open heart and a mind free from judgment. Within this space, partners can explore their deepest fears, desires, and needs and lay the groundwork for a resolution that addresses not just the symptoms but the root cause of their conflicts.

Visual Element: Conflict Roots Diagram

A helpful tool for couples is creating a Conflict Roots Diagram. This visual tool involves drawing a tree, with each branch representing a recurring conflict or disagreement. The roots of the tree are then labeled with potential underlying issues or unmet needs that may be fueling these conflicts. By visually mapping the connections between surface disputes and deeper issues, couples can gain insights into the dynamics of their conflicts and guide their efforts to address the foundational problems.

This diagram serves not only as a tool for understanding but also as a reminder of the complexity of conflicts and the importance of addressing them at their roots. It encourages a shift in perspective from viewing conflicts as obstacles to seeing them as opportunities for growth and deeper connection.

In the garden of a relationship, conflicts, like weeds, are inevitable. Yet, with the right tools and a willingness to dig deep, couples can transform these conflicts into fertile soil for understanding, empathy, and lasting connection. The identification and addressing of the root causes of conflicts stand as the first step in this transformative process, turning points of contention into pathways to a stronger, more resilient bond.

Conflict Resolution Styles and Strategies

In the network of human interaction, the way individuals approach disagreement plays a crucial role in the dynamics of their relationships. Partners, each bearing their own unique blueprint of conflict resolution inherited and honed through a lifetime of personal experiences, often find themselves at a crossroads when their paths of dispute resolution diverge. This divergence, far from being a deadlock, presents an opportunity for a harmonious blend of styles, fostering a dynamic that not only navigates conflicts with grace but also cultivates a deeper understanding and respect for one another's inherent approaches to problem-solving.

The first stride toward this harmonious blend involves an in-depth exploration and acknowledgment of each partner's natural conflict resolution style. One might lean toward a more assertive approach, addressing disagreements head-on with the aim of swift resolution. The other might prefer a more reflective and accommodating style, prioritizing harmony and emotional connection. The recognition and appreciation of these differences are foundational, setting the stage for a relationship where diverse strategies are not points of contention but strengths to be leveraged. It is through this lens that the journey toward effective problem-solving begins, a path marked by mutual respect and the shared goal of achieving outcomes beneficial to both parties.

The transition to a collaborative approach to conflicts, anchored in this mutual respect, requires not just an openness to adapt but also a commitment to adopt strategies that bridge differing styles. This collaborative approach, characterized by its focus on finding solutions that honor both partners' needs and concerns, demands a departure from the realm of win-lose scenarios. Instead, it ventures into a space where compromise and negotiation are not seen as concessions but as steps toward a resolution that embodies the essence of partnership. Techniques such as active listening, where each partner is given the space and freedom to express their perspective without interruption, and empathetic acknowledgment, where the validity of each other's emotions and viewpoints is recognized, are instrumental in this process. These techniques lay the groundwork for an environment where dialogue flourishes, free from the barriers of defensiveness and misunderstanding.

The art of compromising, a cornerstone of this collaborative approach, is refined through practice and patience. It involves a delicate balancing act where the desires and needs of both partners are weighed and honored to the greatest extent possible. This balancing act is facilitated by a clear articulation of non-negotiables, aspects that one or both partners deem critical to their well-being or values, alongside areas where flexibility exists. The negotiation process then becomes an exercise in creativity, exploring various scenarios and solutions that accommodate these core needs while offering concessions in less critical areas. It is a process marked by give-and-take, a collaborative dialogue where solutions are carefully crafted, ensuring that the outcome reflects a shared vision of fairness and mutual satisfaction.

To aid couples in refining their conflict resolution skills, practical exercises serve as both a mirror and map, reflecting current dynamics while guiding the development of new strategies. One such exercise involves role reversal, where partners adopt each other's perspective and articulate the other's position and concerns during a mock conflict. This simple exercise offers profound insights into the emotional landscape of one's partner, fostering empathy and understanding. Another exercise, the creation of a conflict resolution plan, encourages partners to outline steps for addressing disagreements, from the initial recognition of a conflict to the strategies for de-escalation and resolution. This plan revisited regularly, becomes a tangible tool for managing disputes and a reminder of the commitment to resolve conflicts in a manner that strengthens rather than erodes the bond.

In the world of love and partnership, conflicts are inevitable, yet the way they are addressed holds the power either to diminish or deepen the connection between individuals. The exploration and blending of conflict resolution styles, the transition to a collaborative approach, and the adoption of compromise and negotiation as tools for problem-solving are steps on a path toward a relationship where conflicts serve not as standoffs but as opportunities for growth. Through understanding, respect, and the deliberate practice of effective resolution strategies, couples can transform the outlook of their relationship, crafting a dynamic where love thrives not in spite of but because of the challenges faced together.

The Importance of Apology and Forgiveness

In the subtle dynamics of human connection, the steps of apology and forgiveness play a pivotal role, a choreography that demands both grace and courage. Within the sanctum of a relationship, the act of genuine apology and the grace of forgiveness are not mere social niceties but profound gestures of love and respect. They are the balm that heals the wounds of conflict, the bridge that mends the rifts torn open by misunderstanding or hurt. This intricate process begins not with a simple "I'm sorry" but with a deep, introspective understanding of the harm caused, an acknowledgment that lays bare the heart of the transgressor to the light of scrutiny and remorse.

The anatomy of an effective apology is complex, comprising elements that extend far beyond the superficial acknowledgment of wrongdoing. The first of these elements is the acknowledgment of harm, a verbalization that does more than recognize the act itself—it validates the feelings of the injured party, affirming their hurt is both seen and understood. This acknowledgment acts as a key; it unlocks the door to emotional healing by allowing the injured party to feel recognized in their pain.

Closely following this acknowledgment is the expression of genuine regret, a sentiment that resonates with the depth of understanding regarding the impact of the action. This regret is more than just words; it is a heartfelt expression of sorrow for both the action taken and the pain it has caused. It is a subtle element that infuses empathy into the apology, demonstrating an emotional awareness of the partner's distress.

At the core of a meaningful apology is a genuine commitment to change, a forward-looking pledge that the harmful action will not set a pattern for future behavior. This commitment signifies a willingness to engage in self-reflection and undertake the necessary work to alter behavioral patterns. It transforms the apology from a simple acknowledgment into a dynamic promise of personal growth and relationship improvement.

The process of forgiveness is a journey that requires those wronged to demonstrate a deep generosity of spirit. Forgiveness is not an act of forgetting, nor is it a passive acceptance of wrongdoing. Rather, it is an active choice to release the hold of resentment, a decision not to allow past hurt to dictate the emotional climate of the present. This process is facilitated by an understanding of the nature of forgiveness, recognizing it as a pathway to emotional liberation and relationship renewal.

Cultivating a culture of forgiveness within the relationship necessitates an environment where vulnerability is not only accepted but embraced. It requires creating a space where both partners feel safe expressing their deepest hurts and extending the olive branch of forgiveness without fear of rebuke or dismissal. This environment is fostered through consistent empathy, dialogues that prioritize understanding over judgment, and a mutual commitment to nurturing a relationship that values growth and healing.

Advice on the delicate process of apology and forgiveness often centers on open communication, a key principle that is essential for the success of both. Initiating a conversation with the intent to apologize involves not just the readiness to speak but the preparedness to listen, to truly hear, and to absorb the impact of one's actions on the partner. This dialogue, though fraught with emotional vulnerability, is the crucible in which the gold of deeper connection is refined.

Similarly, offering forgiveness is not a unilateral declaration but a mutual exchange. This interaction acknowledges the efforts of the apologizing partner and affirms the injured party's right to emotional healing. This exchange, marked by sincerity and humility, paves the way for rebuilding trust and strengthening the bond.

In the context of love and commitment, where perfection is an illusion, the acts of apology and forgiveness demonstrate the resilience of the human heart. They acknowledge our flaws and celebrate our capacity for empathy, understanding, and growth. By thoughtfully applying these acts, couples can navigate their inevitable conflicts and transform moments of hurt into opportunities for healing and connection. These complex and challenging processes are the building blocks of a lasting, loving relationship.

Creating a Safe Space for Difficult Discussions

In the maze of human emotions, where words can heal or wound, creating a safe space for open dialogue becomes essential. This sanctuary, a place of empathy and respect, plays a pivotal role in a relationship, especially when dealing with the challenges of conflict. Within this space, partners find the courage to open up, comforted by the understanding and support that surrounds them. Here, in this sacred space, honesty flourishes, liberated by the fear of judgment or reprisal, fostering an atmosphere where even the most contentious issues can be addressed with dignity and care.

The architecture of this haven rests on the bedrock of intentional design, a conscious effort to create a domain where the norms of everyday interaction are elevated to a higher standard of empathy and attentiveness. The air within this space is charged with a mutual commitment to protecting the openness of vulnerable hearts and a promise to handle disagreements with a sense of mutual respect. This undertaking begins not with grand gestures but with the subtle art of setting parameters that honor the sanctity of dialogue, ensuring that even in the midst of turmoil, the thread of connection remains unbroken.

The establishment of ground rules for discussions acts as the cornerstone of this sacred space. These mutually agreed-upon rules serve as the framework within which dialogue unfolds, a set of guidelines that guide conversations away from the brink of escalation. They keep the discourse on the path of constructiveness and ensure that there is a shared commitment to understanding and resolution, even in disagreement. Among these rules, the principle of mutual listening stands paramount, a mandate that each voice will be given its rightful space without interruption or dismissal. This principle fosters an environment where each partner, secure in the knowledge that their perspective will be heard, is more likely to approach discussions with openness and sincerity.

Another key rule involves the prohibition of absolutes in language—words like "always" and "never"—that generalize and exacerbate conflicts. Their exclusion encourages a focus on specifics, on the tangible aspects of disagreement that can be addressed and resolved. This shift from hyperbole to precision aids in dissecting conflicts and allows partners to tackle issues with clarity and focus.

A third guideline centers on the recognition of emotional thresholds, an understanding that there are moments when the intensity of feelings may necessitate a pause in the conversation. Acknowledging that emotions may cloud judgment and hinder productive dialogue underscores the importance of taking breaks when needed. These pauses are not retreats; they are strategic intermissions and opportunities to regroup emotionally. They ensure that when the conversation resumes, it will do so from a place of calm and readiness.

In the orchestration of effective communication during tense situations, strategies that transcend the mere articulation of words play a critical role. The strategic use of silence, for instance, serves as a powerful tool, providing a momentary respite from the whirlwind of emotions and a space for reflection and contemplation. Similarly, the practice of paraphrasing, of reflecting back on what has been heard, acts as a mirror, ensuring that understanding is not lost in the transmission of words. This technique not only validates the speaker's sentiments but also fortifies the bridge of understanding, reinforcing the connection at the heart of the dialogue.

Expressions of gratitude and recognition during discussions help ease tensions that arise in moments of disagreement. These simple yet profound expressions remind us of the love and respect that underpin the relationship, counterbalancing the tensions of conflict. They imbue the conversation with a sense of gratitude, recognizing the partner's willingness to engage in the challenging work of resolution.

Moreover, the physical environment in which these discussions take place contributes significantly to the atmosphere of safety and openness. A setting chosen for its tranquility and comfort, away from the distractions of daily life, becomes a physical manifestation of the safe space for dialogue. Whether it's a secluded corner of a home or a serene outdoor setting, it plays a subtle yet impactful role in facilitating open, honest communication.

In the quest to foster a relationship marked by depth and resilience, creating a safe space for difficult discussions reflects the strength of commitment and love. It is a tangible expression of the desire not just to coexist but to thrive, to transform conflicts from obstacles into opportunities for growth and understanding. Through the meticulous crafting of this space, guided by thoughtfully established ground rules and strategies for effective communication, couples move through the complexities of their shared journey with grace and unity, ensuring that even in the face of disagreement, the bonds of empathy and respect remain unbroken.

Preventing Escalation: Tips and Techniques

The potential to transform a spark into a fire looms large in the crucible of conflict. Recognizing and mitigating triggers, those seemingly harmless comments or actions that can unexpectedly fan the flames is paramount in maintaining the equilibrium of discourse. This preemptive approach allows partners to circumvent the pathways leading to heightened tension and steer their interactions toward a harbor of constructive dialogue, even amid the storm.

Strategies for calming down and taking breaks during heated discussions are not merely tactical retreats but essential maneuvers in the choreography of conflict resolution. These strategies hinge on the ability to detect the rising tide of emotions, a perceptual acuity that enables the timely intervention of a pause. A mutual understanding that pauses are acts of preservation, not signals of disengagement, strengthens both partners' resolve to employ them. The architecture of these breaks, structured with clear intentions and durations, ensures that they serve their purpose without giving rise to feelings of abandonment or unresolved tension.

Central to this dance of de-escalation is the art of emotional self-regulation, which demands not just the awareness of one's emotional state but the mastery over one's expressions. Emotional self-regulation, in this context, is akin to the skilled navigator in turbulent seas who maintains the course and guides the ship back to calm waters. It encompasses techniques from deep breathing to reframing negative thoughts and tools that equip individuals to modulate their responses, transforming potential reactions into measured responses.

Practical tips for de-escalating conflicts and returning to a constructive dialogue are manifold, each offering a pathway to re-establishing connection. One approach involves intentionally lowering one's voice, a physical manifestation of calm that can have a contagious effect, diffusing tension. Another technique is the use of humor, not as a means of dismissal but as a gentle release valve for pressure. Laughter can shift the emotional climate, allowing for a return to dialogue from a place of lightness. Additionally, expressing a desire to understand and resolve, even amid disagreement, acts as a beacon, a reminder of the shared goal that transcends the conflict at hand.

In the complex nature of human relationships, the ability to address conflicts with a focus on prevention and de-escalation demonstrates the strength of the connection. It reflects a mutual commitment to the health of the relationship, a recognition that the bonds of love and respect are precious and warrant protection. Through the thoughtful application of strategies for recognizing triggers—employing breaks, practicing emotional self-regulation, and utilizing techniques for calming and re-engagement—partners fortify their union, ensuring that even in disagreement, their respect and care for each other remain undiminished.

Conflicts, while unavoidable, are part of a relationship's complexity and provide not just challenges but opportunities to deepen understanding, strengthen bonds, and reaffirm commitment. The strategies and techniques discussed here serve as tools for couples to manage the complexities of disagreement, fostering a deeper connection and mutual respect. They underscore the importance of mastering the art of conflict resolution, which enriches the relationship and fills it with resilience and grace.

As we draw the curtains on this exploration of conflict resolution, we are reminded of the transformative power of thoughtful engagement in the face of disagreement. The journey through conflict, marked by the strategies of prevention, de-escalation, and resolution, is not a detour but a vital passage in the journey of love and partnership. It is through this passage that the relationship emerges not just intact but invigorated, ready to face the challenges and joys that lie ahead.

Make a Difference with Your Review

"Kindness is like a boomerang—it always comes back to you."

Unknown

Hey there,

You know, sometimes a small act of kindness can change someone's whole day. Or even their entire life! That's why I'm reaching out to you.

Would you be willing to do something amazing today that costs nothing but a minute of your time?

Imagine a couple out there—just like you, once upon a time —looking for guidance, longing for a happier, healthier marriage but unsure where to turn. That's where you come in.

By leaving a review for 'The Practical Guide to a Healthy Marriage,' you're not just giving feedback. You're extending a helping hand to someone who needs it. Your words could be the inspiration they've been waiting for, the nudge they need to start their journey to lasting happiness together. Your review could be the turning point in another couple's life.

It's easy. Just take a moment to scan the QR code below and share your thoughts on the book:

It's a small gesture with a significant impact. And hey, if you believe this book can make a difference for someone else, why not pass it along? Goodwill has a way of coming back around.

Thank you for being part of something special. Your support means the world to me, and I can't wait to hear what you think of the strategies and tips inside!

Warm regards,

D.S. Loden

PS - Did you know that giving something valuable to someone else makes you even more valuable to them? Spread the love!

SIX

Cultivating Growth: Nurturing Self and Partnership

I n the journey of a shared life, individual aspirations and collective dreams blend to create a vibrant picture filled with the colors of personal and mutual growth. This harmonious blend, where individual flourishing fuels the vitality of the partnership, demands a nuanced balance—a dance of encouragement and support that allows both parties to thrive. Within this dynamic, setting and pursuing personal growth goals emerges as a critical element, a catalyst that propels both individuals and their relationships toward a state of continuous evolution and fulfillment.

Setting and Achieving Personal Growth Goals

Personal growth is the process of evolving in response to life's experiences and challenges, serving as a guiding light for individuals as they maneuver the complexities of both their internal and external worlds. In the context of a relationship, this pursuit of self-improvement and satisfaction assumes a dual significance, serving as a source of personal fulfillment and as a contribution to the health of the partnership. The act of setting personal growth goals, therefore, is not a solitary endeavor but a collaborative venture where one's aspirations resonate with and are supported by the other.

Strategies for Setting Realistic and Meaningful Personal Growth Goals

At the outset, formulating personal growth goals requires a deep dive into the self, an introspective journey that uncovers the aspirations lying dormant beneath the surface of daily routines and responsibilities. This exploration, guided by questions of passion, purpose, and potential, leads to the identification of goals that are not only attainable but also deeply resonant with the individual's core values and desires. Whether it's mastering a new skill, pursuing a long-held interest, or overcoming a personal challenge, these goals stand as milestones on the path to self-actualization.

In tandem with setting these goals, articulating a detailed and structured plan to achieve them is imperative. This plan outlines the steps necessary to move from aspiration to reality, transforming vague intentions into actionable strategies. It incorporates timelines, resources, and benchmarks for success, providing a roadmap that guides the individual's efforts and tracks their progress.

Techniques for Supporting Each Other's Goals

In a partnership, supporting each other's personal growth goals demonstrates the depth of the bond and the commitment to mutual flourishing. This support manifests in various forms, from providing encouragement and motivation to offering practical assistance and resources. It involves active listening, where the aspirations and challenges of the partner are met with empathy and understanding, and constructive feedback, where insights and suggestions are shared to facilitate progress.

A relatable comparison to this support dynamic can be found in the mutual aid of climbing partners who, though on individual paths up the mountain, remain tethered, ready to offer a steadying hand or an encouraging word. This symbiotic relationship underscores the importance of balance in the partnership, where the pursuit of personal goals is harmonized with the needs and rhythms of the shared life.

Practical Steps for Tracking and Celebrating Personal Achievements

Milestones mark the journey toward personal growth goals, and each achievement reflects the individual's dedication and effort. Recognizing these achievements is crucial for the individual's sense of accomplishment and for the health of the relationship. This recognition can take the form of shared celebrations, where successes are commemorated together, reinforcing the sense of partnership and shared joy in each other's accomplishments.

Visual Element: The Growth Tracker

To facilitate the tracking of personal growth goals and achievements, the creation of a Growth Tracker is recommended. This visual tool, designed as a chart or a digital spreadsheet, allows individuals to record their goals, track their progress, and note their achievements. It serves as a tangible representation of the journey of growth, a visual reminder of the path traveled and the milestones reached.

In cultivating growth within the context of a partnership, the intertwining of personal aspirations and shared dreams creates a rich landscape of possibility. The setting and pursuit of personal growth goals, supported by strategies for realistic goal-setting, techniques for mutual support, and practical steps for tracking and celebrating achievements, stand as pillars of this dynamic. Through the collaborative endeavor of nurturing self and partnership, individuals find personal fulfillment and a deepening of the bond that unites them, a symbol of the transformative power of growth in love and life.

Developing a Couple's Growth Mindset

A mindset oriented toward growth acts as a catalyst for transforming the inevitable challenges of a shared life into stepping stones for deepening the bond between partners. This perspective, rooted in the belief that abilities and understanding can be developed through dedication and hard work, fosters resilience and adaptability, qualities that are essential for managing the complexities of a relationship. Therefore, cultivating a shared growth mindset is not merely beneficial but imperative for couples aspiring to thrive amid the dynamism of life together.

The transition from viewing obstacles as impasses to perceiving them as opportunities requires a shift in perception, a recalibration of the lens through which one views successes and setbacks. The process begins with the mutual acknowledgment that perfection is unattainable and, frankly, undesirable. There will be missteps and misunderstandings, and the key for partners is to reframe them as fertile ground for learning. In this shared laboratory, experiments in communication, empathy, and support yield invaluable insights into the art of loving better.

The enactment of this mindset necessitates activities that encourage reflection, dialogue, and concerted action. Joint reflection, an activity where partners set aside time to ponder and discuss their experiences, challenges, and reactions, serves as a mirror reflecting the growth achieved and the lessons learned. When approached with openness and curiosity, this reflective practice reveals patterns and triggers that offer clues for enhancing interaction and deepening emotional connectivity. It's like gardeners analyzing the season's yield to better prepare for the next; every insight contributes to a more bountiful future harvest.

Goal setting, another pillar in the development of a shared growth mindset, involves identifying objectives that are both personal and mutual. These carefully chosen and articulated goals become beacons that guide the couple's efforts and energies. Setting these objectives, far from a mere administrative task, is a declaration of intent, a tangible manifestation of the couple's commitment to their collective evolution. It mirrors the practices of successful teams setting strategic goals, where the clarity of purpose and unity of direction propel them toward their desired outcomes.

The commitment to continual learning further enriches the cultivation of this mindset. This learning can take various forms, from acquiring new skills that enhance the couple's life to engaging in activities that challenge their perspectives and encourage adaptability. Whether it's learning a new language together to open the door to new cultures and experiences or taking up a sport that demands teamwork and strategy, learning becomes a metaphor for the relationship itself—ever-evolving, endlessly fascinating. This commitment to learning mirrors the ethos of craftsmen, where mastery is seen not as a destination but as a journey marked by continuous improvement and adaptation.

Mutual encouragement, the keystone of this growth-oriented dynamic, is the fuel that powers the engine of personal and shared development. It's the wind beneath the wings of aspiration, the force that propels the couple forward through doubts and challenges. Encouragement in this context transcends mere platitudes; it embodies a genuine belief in each other's potential and steadfast support for their endeavors. It acknowledges effort over outcome and process over perfection. It mirrors the support of a coach who sees potential in an athlete and nurtures it with patience and belief.

The practical application of this mindset is facilitated by establishing rituals and practices that embed growth, learning, and encouragement into the fabric of the relationship.

These practices, ranging from weekly check-ins to celebrate progress and address challenges to setting aside time for joint learning experiences, become the scaffolding upon which the relationship is built and maintained. They act as reminders of the couple's commitment not just to endure but to flourish, not just to coexist but to co-evolve.

The development of a shared growth mindset is an act of deliberate construction, a building of a shared vision that acknowledges the impermanence of the current state and looks forward with anticipation to the possibilities that lie ahead. It is a mindset that embraces change, one that sees an opportunity for strengthening the bond in every challenge and a lesson to be learned in every setback. Through activities that foster reflection, goal-setting, continual learning, and mutual encouragement, couples cultivate a dynamic and fulfilling relationship that is not static but vibrantly alive, not fixed but fluid, capable of weathering the storms and basking in the sunshine of a life shared in love and growth.

Navigating Life Transitions Together

Life transitions, those markers of change both foreseen and unforeseen, present a unique challenge to the fabric of a relationship. These periods of flux—a career shift, the arrival of a child, the quiet descent into retirement—can both unsettle and invigorate the partnership. Within this dynamic interplay of stability and change, strategies for open communication and mutual support find their significance. Moreover, techniques for adapting to new roles and responsibilities become essential tools for ensuring that the essence of the relationship not only endures but flourishes amid the winds of change.

The key to navigating life transitions lies in cultivating open dialogue, which goes beyond simple conversation to include heartfelt expression and attentive listening. It demands not just the sharing of hopes and the voicing of concerns but also the grace of genuinely hearing, of absorbing the essence of a partner's experience without judgment or censure. This rich and multifaceted dialogue becomes a vital connection within the relationship, reinforcing its strength against the potential challenges of transition. It involves articulating individual experiences of change and co-creating a shared narrative, a story of transition that acknowledges the individual while celebrating the collective.

In this shared narrative, acknowledging the emotional landscape of transition is pivotal. It recognizes that change, even when positive or eagerly anticipated, carries with it an emotional weight, an intricate blend of excitement, apprehension, and grief for what is left behind. Addressing this emotional complexity requires a delicate balance, a dance of support that validates feelings without becoming trapped in them. Emotional and practical support becomes the bedrock upon which partners rely, a steadfast presence that anchors the relationship amid the flux of transition.

Techniques for adapting to new roles and responsibilities emerge as a natural extension of this dialogue and support. They involve a reimagining of the partnership, a recalibration of roles that honors the evolving landscape of each partner's world. This adaptation is not a rigid reassignment of tasks but a fluid negotiation, a dynamic process that respects each individual's shifting needs and capacities. It acknowledges that roles within the relationship are not static but responsive to life's changes.

At the heart of this negotiation is the acknowledgment of the value of flexibility and the inherent strength found in adaptability. It champions the idea that resilience is not a product of rigidity but of the capacity to bend without breaking, to adjust, and to realign in response to the changing shape of life's path. This flexibility is not aimless; it is guided by a mutual vision for the relationship and a shared understanding of the values and priorities that anchor the partnership.

Celebrating the milestones within these periods of change and recognizing and appreciating the moments of achievement and challenge are essential for successfully managing transitions. These acts of acknowledgment serve not just as a record of progress but as a reaffirmation of the partnership's resilience and adaptability. They acknowledge that a series of steps, each significant in its contribution to the journey of adaptation, lies within every transition. Whether they are quiet reflections or shared expressions of joy, these celebrations imbue the process of transition with a sense of accomplishment and gratitude, enriching the partnership with a deeper appreciation for the journey taken together.

Embedded within the narrative of life's transitions are individual and collective stories that serve as both a testament and guide to the capacity of relationships to adapt and grow. These stories, drawn from the partners' experiences and from the wisdom of those who have traveled similar paths, offer insights into the challenges and triumphs of adaptation. They remind us that transitions, while inherently disruptive, also hold the potential for profound growth and deepening connection.

Exercises for exploring and understanding these transitions become tools of empowerment, avenues for couples to engage actively with the process of change. Ranging from shared journaling that captures the emotional journey of transition to collaborative planning sessions that map the path through change, these exercises foster a sense of agency. They enable partners to move from being passive witnesses to active participants in their narrative of change, co-authors of their partnership's evolving story.

In the unfolding story of a relationship, life's transitions are rich with the potential for growth, the deepening of bonds, and the expansion of understanding. When combined, the strategies of open communication and mutual support, the techniques for adapting to new roles, and the practices of celebration and reflection form a pattern of growth. They underscore the capacity of partnerships not only to withstand the pressures of change but to emerge, transformed and strengthened, ready to embrace the next horizon with confidence and grace.

Balancing Individuality with Togetherness

The balance between individuality and togetherness is crucial in the complex dynamics of a committed relationship. This harmony, enriched by personal freedom and shared experiences, requires a skilled conductor who can balance distinct melodies so that none overshadows the others. This balance is the key to a thriving relationship—one that respects individual autonomy while being deeply rooted in intimate connection.

The pursuit of personal independence within the framework of a relationship is not a solitary endeavor but a joint venture. It begins with the mutual acknowledgment that the essence of love does not confine but liberates, allowing each partner to explore the vast landscapes of their individuality. This exploration, far from undermining the connection, enriches it, bringing back the treasures discovered on these solo journeys into the partnership. The strategies to achieve this delicate balance involve a blend of communication, understanding, and intentional action, each element integrated with care and consideration.

Communication, the beacon that guides the relationship through the fog of misunderstanding, assumes a pivotal role. It is through communication that partners articulate their needs for personal space and autonomy and frame these needs as avenues for growth, not as retreats from the relationship. This nuanced and ongoing dialogue ensures that both partners feel heard and validated, fostering an atmosphere of trust where individual pursuits are encouraged. It mirrors the precision of a diplomat, where every word is chosen with care, and every sentence is crafted to build bridges rather than walls.

Understanding, the companion of communication, involves a deep empathy for the partner's aspirations and pursuits, one that transcends mere acceptance and delves into the realm of active encouragement. This understanding is not passive but dynamic, engaging with the partner's interests, celebrating their achievements, and offering support in their endeavors. It reflects the wisdom of a sage, recognizing that the growth of the individual contributes to the richness of the shared experience and that in their partner's fulfillment, their joy is also found.

Intentional action, the tangible manifestation of this balance, involves the creation of spaces and opportunities for individual pursuits. It might involve setting aside time for personal hobbies or interests or establishing boundaries that respect personal reflection and solitude. These deliberate and thoughtful actions ensure that the relationship breathes freely and is nurtured by mutual respect and freedom. They echo the strategy of a master gardener who knows that for the garden to thrive, each plant must have the space to grow, the nutrients to flourish, and the support to stand tall.

The role of personal space and autonomy in a healthy relationship cannot be overstated. It is the oxygen that fuels the fire of passion, the soil that nourishes the roots of intimacy. This space, sacred and respected, is the sanctuary where the self is honored, where the whispers of the soul are heeded. In this personal sanctuary, individuals reconnect with their essence and emerge rejuvenated and inspired, ready to engage with the partnership from a place of wholeness and vitality.

Finding the right balance between pursuing individual interests and investing in shared experiences is comparable to the
arrangement of a musical piece. Each note, whether played
solo or in harmony, contributes to the beauty of the piece.
Achieving this balance begins with establishing rituals that
honor both the individual and the couple. These rituals,
whether they be solitary morning walks or shared evening
meals, create a rhythm to the relationship, a cadence that
respects the need for both personal expression and intimate
connection.

Shared experiences, selected with care, provide the canvas on
which the couple paints their shared memories. These experiences, whether adventures in travel, intellectual pursuits, or
creative endeavors, are chosen for their capacity to enrich the
partnership and create a shared narrative that is dynamic and
layered. They are the connections that unite, the colors that
enhance the essence of the relationship. While each partner
embarks on their journey, they return to a shared home
enriched by their adventures.

In the delicate equilibrium of a relationship, the balance
between individuality and togetherness is both a challenge
and an opportunity. It requires flexibility, empathy, and an
unwavering commitment to the growth of both the self and
the partnership. Through strategies that encourage personal
independence alongside emotional connection, through the
cultivation of understanding, and the practice of intentional
action, couples navigate this balance. They ensure that their
relationship, while rooted in the deep soil of shared love and
experience, is always reaching toward the sun, each partner

flourishing in the light of their individuality and the warmth of their togetherness.

Celebrating Milestones and Successes

In the unfolding narrative of a shared existence, moments that mark progress and triumphs, whether monumental or modest, serve as critical chapters. When recognized and celebrated, these instances act not merely as reflections of achievements but as affirmations of the journey undertaken together. They stand as beacons, illuminating the path trodden and the one that stretches ahead, reinforcing the unity and purpose that propels the partnership forward. The act of commemorating these milestones and successes adopts a dual significance, enriching the relationship with layers of meaning and memories while also fortifying the bonds that connect hearts together.

The initiation of traditions for commemorating special occasions and achievements emerges as a pivotal ritual in a couple's life. These traditions, personalized and filled with personal significance, turn the celebration into a sacred ritual, reflecting the values and shared experiences that define the partnership. Whether it's an annual getaway to reminisce and set intentions for the year ahead or a simple, intimate ceremony where letters of appreciation and dreams for the future are exchanged, these traditions become the milestones themselves, markers of time and evidence of growth. They serve as reminders of past successes and sources of motivation and excitement for the adventures that lie ahead.

The role of gratitude and appreciation in a relationship cannot be overstated. It is the crucible in which the ordinary is transmuted into the sublime, where daily acts of kindness and support are recognized as the extraordinary gestures they truly are. The expression of gratitude, therefore, becomes a vital thread in the fabric of celebrations, elevating them from mere events to profound acknowledgments of each partner's role in the collective journey. Techniques for integrating gratitude into these celebrations might include creating a shared gratitude journal to highlight the moments of support and sacrifice that often go unnoticed. Another idea is to use a gratitude jar filled throughout the year with notes of thanks and appreciation, which can be opened and reflected upon during a designated celebration. These simple yet profound practices anchor the relationship in an ethos of mutual respect and admiration; they ensure that no achievement, no matter how minor it may seem, goes unrecognized.

Creating rituals and traditions that celebrate the couple's growth and accomplishments requires an investment of creativity and intent. These rituals, far from being predictable, reflect the unique journey of each partnership, tailored to the narratives and dreams shaping the couple's shared life. They might involve revisiting the place where significant milestones in the relationship were reached, reenacting a moment of triumph, or creating a piece of art that captures the essence of their journey together. These acts of celebration, woven into the rhythm of the relationship, become touchstones, reminders of the path walked together and the terrain yet to be explored.

Furthermore, integrating these celebratory practices into the foundation of the relationship serves as a safeguard against the erosion of connection that time and familiarity can bring. They act as renewals of the commitment and love that form the foundation of the partnership, invigorating the bond with fresh energy and reinforcing the notion that together, the individuals are greater than the sum of their parts. It is through these celebrations that the couple reaffirms their dedication to each other and to the continuous cultivation of a partnership that is vibrant, evolving, and deeply rooted in mutual respect and admiration.

In this landscape of shared existence, celebrating milestones and successes emerges as a vital element in the architecture of a fulfilling relationship. Through these moments of acknowledgment and appreciation, the partnership is nourished and sustained, ensuring that the journey together, with all its challenges and triumphs, is marked not by the milestones themselves but by the depth of connection and understanding that these celebrations foster. As we integrate these practices of recognition, gratitude, and tradition into our relationship, we strengthen the bonds that unite us and ensure that our partnership remains a source of strength, joy, and unending growth.

As this chapter blends into the fabric of our shared story, the essence of celebrating milestones and successes becomes clear. This reflects the power of recognition and appreciation in the essence of love. It beckons us forward, not just as partners but as co-creators of a journey rich with meaning, woven with the threads of gratitude, tradition, and shared triumphs.

SEVEN

Enhancing Communication Through Practice

I n the vast landscape of human interaction, the act of listening, truly listening, stands as a beacon of connection. It goes beyond just exchanging words to foster understanding and empathy. Amid the noise of daily life, where distractions abound, and minds wander, the art of active listening emerges not as a given but as a skill to be honed, a discipline to be cultivated with intention and care. This chapter delves into the realm of active listening exercises, offering strategies for couples to bridge the chasms of miscommunication and nurture a garden where every word and sentiment is both heard and felt.

Active Listening Exercises

At its core, active listening is an act of surrendering to another person's words and emotions, setting aside one's own thoughts and judgments to fully immerse oneself in the partner's message. It requires a dedication to presence that is all too rare in an age of perpetual motion and distraction. The exercises presented here are designed to sharpen this skill and transform listening into a sanctuary of empathy and understanding within the relationship.

Mirroring, Paraphrasing, and Summarizing

At the heart of active listening lie the techniques of mirroring, paraphrasing, and summarizing. Mirroring involves repeating the speaker's words verbatim, a reflection that assures the speaker they have been heard. Paraphrasing goes a step further, rewording the speaker's message in the listener's own words—a sign of understanding. Summarizing draws together the main points of what has been said, offering a concise depiction of the conversation's essence. Together, these techniques serve as the pillars of active listening, each reinforcing the bond of communication and empathy.

Imagine a quiet evening at home when one partner expresses frustration about their day. The other, practicing mirroring, repeats the sentiments shared and then paraphrases the frustrations, offering their interpretation of what they've heard. Finally, they summarize the conversation, encapsulating the key points of the discussion. This exercise, simple in its execution, deepens the connection, ensuring both partners feel valued and understood.

Listening Without Interrupting and Validating Feelings

A foundational aspect of active listening is the ability to listen without interrupting and to offer space for the partner's words without the interjection of one's own thoughts or solutions. This silence is not passive; it is an active engagement with the speaker's message, an affirmation of its value. Coupled with this is the practice of validating feelings and acknowledging the emotions conveyed without judgment or diminishment. Such validation is a balm to the soul, a recognition of the legitimacy of the partner's emotional experience.

Consider setting aside time each day for uninterrupted listening, a moment when phones are silenced and distractions are set aside. In this space, one partner shares while the other listens entirely and without interruption, then offers validation of the feelings expressed. This ritual, woven into the fabric of daily life, becomes a cornerstone of empathy and understanding, a daily reaffirmation of the partnership's depth.

Creating a Safe Space for Communication

The culmination of active listening exercises is the creation of a safe space for communication, an environment where vulnerability is not just protected but cherished. This sanctuary of dialogue is built on the practices of mirroring, paraphrasing, summarizing, and validating, each contributing to an atmosphere of trust and openness. In this space, partners are free to express their deepest hopes, fears, and desires, confident that they will be received with empathy and understanding.

Establishing this safe space might involve the designation of a specific place in the home that is free from the interruptions of daily life. In this corner, conversation flows freely, and listening is the currency of connection. In this space, active listening exercises are practiced, not as tasks to be checked off but as offerings of love and respect.

Interactive Element: Active Listening Workbook

An Active Listening Workbook is provided to facilitate the practice of these exercises. This workbook includes guided exercises for mirroring, paraphrasing, and summarizing, along with prompts for practicing listening without interruption and validating feelings. It serves as a tangible tool for couples to explore the nuances of active listening, offering a structured approach to enhancing their communication skills. Through reflection sections and resource lists, the workbook guides couples on their journey toward deeper empathy and understanding, making the acts of listening and communicating not just habits but hallmarks of their relationship.

Within love and connection, where words serve as bridges between us, active listening highlights the importance of presence and empathy. Through the exercises outlined in this chapter, couples embark on a path of enhanced communication, transforming the act of listening into an art form, a sacred exchange that nurtures the heart of the relationship.

Expressing Needs Without Blame

In the complex nature of a relationship, clearly expressing our needs and desires is crucial for building strength and resilience. This act, seemingly straightforward, is often entangled in the fear of vulnerability, the apprehension of rejection, or the shadow of past misunderstandings. Within this complex interplay of emotions and expectations, the skill of articulating needs without casting blame emerges as an anchor for nurturing a dialogue rooted in respect and mutual comprehension. This segment explores exercises and methodologies designed to refine this skill, transforming communication into a conduit for deeper empathy and connection.

At the core of this exploration lies the practice of utilizing "I" statements, a linguistic tool that shifts the focus from an accusatory stance to one of personal expression and responsibility. This subtle yet profound adjustment in language structure fosters an environment where defensiveness is minimized and openness flourishes. By framing sentiments and requests from the perspective of one's feelings and experiences, the door to understanding swings wide, inviting a response rooted in compassion rather than resistance. The delicacy of this approach masks its strength; it is like moving through a complex maze with a strand of silk – gentle yet unbreakable, guiding both speaker and listener toward a clearing of mutual respect.

Exercises that encourage the regular use of "I" statements are introduced to embed this practice into the fibers of the relationship. These exercises vary in form but share a common goal – to recalibrate the way needs are voiced to ensure that the emphasis remains on self-expression rather than accusation. One such exercise involves partners sharing thoughts about a neutral topic using only "I" statements, gradually escalating to more emotionally charged subjects. This progression, carefully moderated, allows for the naturalization of this communicative approach, embedding it into the couple's interactional DNA.

Complementing the use of "I" statements, role-playing scenarios stand as a dynamic and interactive means to hone the skill of expressing needs without blame. These scenarios, crafted with care to reflect the nuances and challenges specific to each relationship, provide a safe arena for experimentation and learning. Partners alternate roles, engaging in both scripted and spontaneous dialogues that mirror real-life situations. This experiential learning, grounded in the immediacy of practice, sharpens the ability to communicate needs clearly and respectfully, adjusting tone and wording to fit the moment's emotional landscape. The feedback loop inherent in these role-playing exercises serves as a mirror, reflecting both missteps and triumphs and guiding partners toward a more empathetic and effective mode of expression.

Central to the refinement of this communicative skill is the awareness and avoidance of accusatory language, a common pitfall that can derail conversations into the territory of conflict and misunderstanding. Tips for recognizing and circumventing this language provide a foundation for supportive dialogue. Partners are encouraged to remain vigilant for phrases and tones that hint at blame and to replace them with expressions that focus on personal feelings and experiences. Paired with the commitment to constructive and supportive communication, this vigilance acts as a bulwark against the erosion of dialogue by the corrosive effects of blame.

Addressing the complexities of expressing needs without blame demands the mastery of specific linguistic tools and exercises and a foundation of trust and mutual respect. It is upon this foundation that effective communication is established, each brick laid with care, and each room designed to house the countless expressions of human needs and desires. Through diligent practice and a shared commitment to understanding, couples can transform their dialogue and ensure that every need voiced is an opportunity for connection rather than contention.

The Power of Appreciation in Daily Interactions

In the complex web of marital communication, expressions of appreciation, made with care and intention, enhance and strengthen the union. This fabric, enriched with daily affirmations of gratitude, becomes a resilient shield against the wear and tear of routine and the unpredictable storms of life. The act of expressing appreciation, far from a mere polite gesture, is a profound communication of recognition and value, a signal that one's partner's efforts, characteristics, and essence are not only noticed but deeply cherished.

Incorporating regular expressions of appreciation into the dialect of a relationship demands a shift from passive acknowledgment to active engagement. It invites couples to adopt a lens of gratitude through which the daily actions, sacrifices, and gestures of love that often fade into the background of familiarity are brought into sharp, vibrant focus. This shift, subtle in its execution, is revolutionary in its impact, transforming the mundane into the extraordinary and the expected into the celebrated.

Activities designed to cultivate this habit of appreciation take various forms, each tailored to fit the unique rhythm and language of the relationship. One such activity involves the deliberate identification and verbalization of aspects of one's partner to be grateful for, a practice that can be seamlessly integrated into the rhythm of daily life. Whether it's over morning coffee or a quiet moment before sleep, taking turns articulating specific appreciations offers a moment of connection. This verbal embrace envelops both the giver and the receiver in warmth and recognition.

Exercises extend beyond the spoken word to embrace the tactile and the visual in creative displays of gratitude. Handwritten notes strategically placed where they can surprise and delight—tucked into a lunch bag, left on a pillow, or affixed to a bathroom mirror—serve as tangible reminders of affection and appreciation. These notes, small in size but monumental in significance, act as whispers of love, bridging distances and busy schedules with the intimacy of penned words.

Spontaneous compliments, another facet of this practice, inject moments of joy and validation into the ordinary. These compliments are gifts of pure, unadulterated appreciation, free from the constraints of special occasions or prompted reciprocation. They acknowledge the beauty, effort, and uniqueness of one's partner in real time, turning a fleeting moment into a cherished memory. The spontaneity of these compliments mirrors the unpredictable nature of joy, reminding us that appreciation, like happiness, flourishes in the soil of spontaneity.

Building a positive communication cycle through these practices creates a self-reinforcing loop of appreciation and affection. Each expression of gratitude becomes a brick in the foundation of the relationship, and each act of recognition is a thread that pulls the partners closer. Once initiated, this cycle gains momentum, transforming the relationship into a dynamic ecosystem in which appreciation leads to more appreciation, and gratitude is both the sunlight and the water that nourishes the connection.

The impact of this approach on relationship satisfaction and communication is profound and multifaceted. It fosters an atmosphere of positive reinforcement, where the behaviors and qualities that are appreciated are likely to be emphasized and repeated. This reinforcement not only elevates both partners' mood and well-being, but it also acts as a buffer against conflict, creating a reservoir of goodwill that can be drawn upon in times of tension.

Moreover, the practice of expressing appreciation serves as a mirror, reflecting each partner's value and worth through the other's eyes. This reflection, imbued with love and respect, reinforces the bond between partners, anchoring the relationship in a mutual acknowledgment of significance and belonging. Reaffirming the partnership's vitality and importance is a powerful antidote to the feelings of invisibility and neglect that can erode the connection.

In the grand scheme of a shared life, the power of appreciation in daily interactions is both a simple pleasure and a profound investment. It demands little but offers much, a gesture that is easy to give and transformative to receive. Through activities that encourage the identification, verbalization, and creative expression of gratitude, couples build a habit and a culture of appreciation, a climate where love is not just declared but demonstrated in the currency of acknowledgment and appreciation.

This approach to communication, rooted in recognizing and celebrating each other's worth, weaves a beautiful and durable fabric of connection. It creates a relationship in which each day is an opportunity for appreciation, where every interaction is a chance to affirm the other's value. In this landscape of gratitude, love finds its most eloquent expression, not in grand gestures but in the quiet, consistent acts of appreciation that color every day with the hues of joy and satisfaction.

Role-Playing Difficult Conversations

Exploring the challenges of a committed relationship necessitates a readiness to engage in dialogues that, while challenging, are pivotal to the fabric of mutual understanding and respect. Role-playing, a method often relegated to therapy and training, emerges here as a vital instrument for couples intent on refining their communicative prowess. By simulating real-life scenarios within a controlled environment, this method minimizes the trepidation associated with confronting sensitive topics and transforms potential anxiety into a landscape of learning and growth.

Simulating challenging scenarios through role-playing offers partners a mirror to their communicative behaviors, attitudes, and reflexes, often illuminating patterns previously hidden by the intensity of genuine conflict. By stepping into a defined role, individuals gain the freedom to explore responses and tread paths untaken in their interactions. This exploration, though hypothetical, bears the weight of tangible possibilities, offering insights into alternative methods of articulation and understanding. Each scenario, carefully constructed to mirror the intricacies and potential flashpoints of genuine disputes, serves as a crucible for transformation, where the raw materials of habitual communication are refined into the gold of empathetic and assertive dialogue.

Feedback sessions, integral to the role-playing process, provide a space for reflection and recalibration. Approached with an ethos of constructive criticism, these sessions are less about the enumeration of faults and more about identifying opportunities for growth. As partners adopt the dual roles of critic and advocate, they offer insights into the strengths and weaknesses of the other's communicative style. This reciprocal evaluation, grounded in the desire for mutual growth, fosters an environment where feedback is embraced as a catalyst for change. The insights gleaned from these sessions incrementally reshape the relationship's communicative landscape, imbuing it with a greater capacity for empathy, clarity, and resilience.

The ultimate goal of these exercises is to instill confidence in both partners, not only in their ability to handle the storms of difficult conversations but also in their resilience as a unified entity. This confidence, born of practice and reflection, becomes a barrier against misunderstanding and fear. It empowers partners to approach sensitive topics not as minefields to be circumvented but as bridges to deeper understanding, with each conversation presenting an opportunity to reinforce the foundation of their bond.

Handling sensitive topics with empathy and assertiveness, the twin stars by which these exercises navigate, demands a recalibration of perspectives and strategies. Empathy, in this context, is not a passive absorption of the partner's viewpoints but an active engagement with their emotional and logical landscapes, a willingness to inhabit their worldviews without relinquishing one's own. Assertiveness, conversely, is not the imposition of one's perspective but the clear, respectful articulation of one's needs and views, a balancing act between self-advocacy and receptiveness to the other. This duality, the harmonious coexistence of empathy and assertiveness, forms the keystone of effective communication, a principle brought to life through role-playing.

In role-playing, scenarios unfold as samples of potential realities, each offering a glimpse into the dynamics that shape everyday interactions. From discussions on financial planning that tread the fine line between pragmatism and dreams to discussions on parenting that balance individual philosophies with shared goals, these exercises span the spectrum of marital discourse. They probe the depths of topics like intimacy and personal growth, where vulnerabilities surface and the need for understanding and support is most acute. These scenarios offer partners a panoramic view of their relationship's communicative landscape, an opportunity to survey its contours and identify areas ripe for cultivation and growth.

This methodological approach to refining communication offers more than just the promise of enhanced dialogue; it embodies a commitment to the continual evolution of the partnership. It acknowledges that the path to mutual understanding and respect is not linear but cyclical, a journey of constant learning and adaptation. In this context, role-playing is not just an exercise; it demonstrates the resilience of love and its ability to endure and thrive amid the challenges of living together.

In the delicate dynamics of a relationship, where every step and misstep influences the connection, role-playing difficult conversations provides partners with the tools to communicate effectively and gracefully. It symbolizes their dedication to the craft of understanding, which, like any other craft, requires patience, practice, and the courage to confront the unknown. Through this practice, couples forge a language of love that is not just spoken but lived, where empathy and assertiveness are the dialects of deep connection.

Developing a Personal Communication Plan

In a shared existence, dialogue is the vital force that binds a relationship, providing resilience and flexibility. Developing a personalized communication plan is like creating a map for managing the ups and downs of a partnership and guiding partners through the complexities of daily life and the challenges of conflict. This plan, crafted from daily interaction, conflict resolution, and mutual growth, becomes a living document that evolves alongside the relationship, reflecting the dynamic nature of human connection.

At its inception, this plan demands quiet introspection, allowing couples to examine their communication styles and identify the gems of effective dialogue as well as the pitfalls of misunderstanding. This process lays the groundwork for creating a blueprint that addresses the unique needs of each partner, combining aspirational goals with the practical realities of their shared life. The development of this plan is a collaborative effort, a dialogue within a dialogue that reinforces the foundation of mutual understanding and respect.

The cornerstone of this communication plan rests on the daily exchanges that form the rhythm of the relationship's heartbeat. Here, the focus sharpens on the quality of interaction, the infusion of active listening, and the expression of appreciation. Strategies for enhancing these daily interactions include designated moments of undivided attention and establishing rituals of gratitude that transform the ordinary into the extraordinary. The goal is to enhance daily interactions by turning routine exchanges into chances for connection and affirmation.

In facing the turbulent waters of conflict, the plan charts a course that steers clear of the pitfalls of accusation and defensiveness, guiding couples toward the open seas of resolution and understanding. It outlines techniques for de-escalating tensions, such as taking timeouts to the strategic employment of "I" statements that express needs without casting blame.

This part of the plan serves as a safeguard against the storms of disagreement, offering protocols that ensure safe passage through challenging moments.

Supporting each other's growth becomes a crucial element of this plan, acknowledging that individual development nurtures the relationship's health. This section outlines strategies for fostering personal and mutual development, from setting shared goals to celebrating individual achievements. It recognizes that the journey of growth is both a solitary and a shared endeavor, and it crafts a vision for a partnership that thrives on the enrichment of each member.

Templates and tools, from worksheets that guide the articulation of daily communication goals to checklists for conflict resolution strategies, serve as helpful guides on this journey. These instruments are designed to be revisited and revised, reflecting the plan's living nature. They are markers of progress, reminders of the journey's milestones, and beacons for the path ahead.

Emphasis is placed on the importance of setting realistic goals. The dynamics of a relationship are constantly changing, and flexibility is key to adapting to these shifts. This flexibility allows the plan to breathe, expand, and contract in response to the partnership's evolving dynamics. Regular revisitation of the plan is encouraged. Reflection ensures its relevance and effectiveness, making it a guiding resource for the couple's evolving needs and aspirations.

In the grand design of a relationship, a personalized communication plan is both a compass and a map, a resource that assists couples in handling the difficulties of daily interaction and the challenges of conflict toward the shores of mutual growth and understanding. It showcases the power of intentional dialogue, a reminder that the strength of a partnership lies not in the absence of conflict but in the ability to communicate with clarity, empathy, and respect.

This carefully crafted and thoughtfully maintained plan reflects the couple's journey, documenting their challenges, triumphs, and the depth of their connection. It is a declaration of commitment not only to preserving their bond but also to nurturing its growth. It is a pledge to approach the complexities of their shared life with intention, understanding, and unwavering dedication to each other.

As we conclude this exploration, we are reminded of the transformative power of communication in relationship chemistry. Developing a personalized communication plan is not an end but a beginning, a first step on the path to a deeper, more resilient partnership. It is a journey marked by the willingness to listen, the courage to speak, and the commitment to grow together. Though filled with challenges, it is rich with the rewards of connection and understanding.

EIGHT

Trust Reinforced Through Shared Endeavors

In the delicate ecosystem of a relationship, trust and connection are like water and sunlight— indispensable to its nurturing and growth. Yet, in the bustling rhythm of daily life, the sustenance of trust can be overlooked, its quiet importance drowned out by the noise of immediate needs. Within this context, weekly trust-building challenges emerge, not as a remedy but as a proactive cultivation of the soil in which the relationship thrives. These challenges, varied and intentional, serve as raindrops, each contributing to the reservoir of trust that sustains the partnership through drought and flood.

Weekly Trust-Building Challenges

At the heart of trust lie the dual principles of vulnerability and reliability, the former inviting openness, the latter demanding consistency. The interplay between these forces creates a dynamic tension, a balance that, when maintained, fosters a deepening of connection. Weekly trust-building challenges, which offer couples a structured yet flexible framework to explore and reinforce their trust in one another, are designed to engage these principles.

The challenges range from small acts of kindness, like preparing a surprise breakfast on a dreary Monday morning, to sharing personal fears or dreams, such as a desire to change careers or anxiety about an upcoming family gathering. Regardless of its scale, each challenge is an invitation to show up for the partner with actions and words affirming commitment and care.

Setting up these challenges requires a collaborative approach, a discussion that acknowledges the uniqueness of the relationship and the specific areas where trust can be fortified. Couples might choose to write down ideas and then select one challenge per week, ensuring a mix of simplicity and depth, lightheartedness and seriousness. Following through, then, becomes a shared responsibility, a pact to prioritize these small yet significant gestures, marking them on the calendar as one would an important meeting or family event.

Tracking progress is essential to recognizing the impact of these challenges on the relationship. A shared journal or digital document can serve as a repository of reflections, a space where both partners document their feelings before and after each challenge, noting the shifts in perception, the deepening of trust, and the strengthening of connection. Over time, this record becomes a celebration of the couple's journey, a map showing where they've been and how far they've come.

The encouragement of vulnerability and reliability in these weekly challenges is the sunlight and water the relationship needs to grow. It is deliberate nurturing, a choice to invest in the foundational elements of trust and ensure that the bond between partners is not just maintained but enriched.

Visual Element: Trust Building Challenge Tracker

A Trust Building Challenge Tracker, visually structured as a calendar, offers couples a tangible tool to plan, execute, and reflect on their weekly challenges. This tracker, which can be printed or digitally maintained, features spaces for noting the challenge of the week, the intended outcome, and personal reflections on the experience. Accompanied by symbols or colors to represent different types of challenges — acts of kindness, shared vulnerabilities, expressions of gratitude — this tool both organizes the endeavor and makes it engaging, a visual reminder of the commitment to fortify the relationship.

In the shared journey of life, trust is the foundation that links every interaction, shaping both moments of connection and instances of misunderstanding. It is both the starting point and the destination, the question and the answer. Through the practice of weekly trust-building challenges, couples step into a rhythm of engagement with the principles of vulnerability and reliability, crafting a relationship that not only endures but thrives. This endeavor, marked by small acts and shared dreams, becomes a dance of trust, a mutual journey toward a deeper, more resilient bond.

Intimacy-Boosting Activities for Every Couple

Amid the daily interactions that shape a relationship, the bonds of intimacy can sometimes loosen or tangle, overshadowed by routine and diminished by familiarity. The endeavor to maintain, and indeed elevate, intimacy within the partnership calls for a deliberate infusion of effort and creativity, a conscious act of weaving new patterns that invigorate and strengthen the bond. This section presents a collection of activities designed to enrich the various aspects of emotional, physical, and experiential intimacy, offering couples a palette to paint their interactions with vibrant hues of connection and discovery.

The foundation of emotional intimacy lies in the profound understanding and sharing of one's inner world, an endeavor that transcends the surface-level exchange of pleasantries and delves into the essence of the soul. To facilitate this deep connection, couples are encouraged to engage in activities that foster vulnerability and empathy. One activity is the practice of "Heart Maps," where partners draw literal or metaphorical maps of their emotional landscapes, marking the terrains of their fears, dreams, and joys, and then share these maps with one another. This mapping of the heart invites exploration and understanding and offers a visual and symbolic guide to each other's inner worlds.

Physical intimacy, often misconceived as merely the sensual domain, encompasses a broader spectrum of touch and closeness, serving as a vital conduit for warmth and affection. This dimension's rejuvenation can be achieved by reintroducing a playful, non-sexual touch into daily interactions. The "Touch

Alphabet" game, where partners spell out words on each other's backs or palms using their fingertips, not only cultivates a tactile language of love but also instills moments of light-hearted connection into the rhythm of the day. While simple, this activity is potent in bringing physical closeness into everyday life, transforming mundane moments into opportunities for tenderness and connection.

Experiential intimacy, the shared journey through the landscapes of life, thrives on novelty and shared endeavors, on the creation of memories that become the milestones of the relationship. To enrich this dimension, couples are invited to embark on "Adventure Quests," a series of planned or spontaneous activities that break the monotony of routine and ignite the spark of discovery. These quests might range from exploring an unfamiliar cuisine to a challenge that combines the joy of learning with the delight of sensory experience to a day spent in nature, where the simplicity of the setting encourages a focus on the moment and on each other. These experiences act as strands of shared joy and curiosity, creating a deeper, more vibrant sense of connection.

In the realm of conversation, the lifeblood of intimacy, introducing "Dialogue Decks" offers a structured yet flexible platform for deepening communication. Composed of cards bearing questions or prompts designed to explore beliefs, experiences, and aspirations, these decks serve as catalysts for conversations that might not arise during daily life. Using these decks during dedicated "Conversation Evenings" transforms dialogue into an event, an anticipated space focused on understanding and connection. By elevating conversation from the incidental to the intentional, this practice reaffirms the primacy of emotional and intellectual intimacy within the partnership.

The continual discovery of one another, a principle that underpins the activities proposed, recognizes that both the self and the relationship are dynamic, ever-evolving entities. The commitment to engage in these intimacy-boosting activities is, therefore, a commitment to growth, to the belief that exploring each other's depths and breadths is not a journey with a destination but a perpetual voyage that enriches and enlivens the relationship. These activities, tailored to the nuances of emotional, physical, and experiential intimacy, provide couples with the tools to not only tackle the challenges of maintaining closeness but also elevate their bond to new heights of understanding and affection.

In the architecture of a relationship, the column of intimacy bears much of the weight of connection and satisfaction. Maintaining this pillar is not a task but a privilege, an opportunity to consistently infuse new layers of closeness and warmth into the partnership. Through deliberate and joyful engagement in activities that boost intimacy, couples can ensure that their bond remains vibrant and robust, showcasing the power of creative effort in pursuing deep, lasting love.

The Trust Talk: Establishing Ground Rules for Honesty

In a committed relationship, the tempo is often set by the rhythm of truth and transparency, guiding the connection between partners. The conversation surrounding honesty, while delicate, is crucial and requires both partners to engage with tact and sensitivity. This nuanced dialogue, essential for building trust, demands a mutual commitment to clarity and vulnerability; it sets the stage for a relationship in which openness flourishes. To ensure this, a mutual exploration to define honesty's form within the partnership becomes imperative. This quest, far from a mere academic exercise, is an intimate journey into each partner's values and expectations, a collaborative effort to sketch the boundaries of their shared landscape of trust. Here, honesty is not a single entity but an elaborate blend, with its nuances and details reflecting the unique qualities of the relationship. Partners engage in a delicate negotiation, voicing their interpretations and listening with an open heart, aiming to construct a shared definition that respects individual perspectives while fostering a collective understanding.

Establishing ground rules for engaging in difficult conversations emerges as a natural progression in this dialogue. These guidelines, carefully developed and mutually agreed upon, act as a support system for discussions that, while potentially filled with emotional challenges, are necessary for the relationship's vitality. Crafting these rules is an exercise in foresight and empathy, anticipating the pitfalls that can derail honest dialogue and agreeing on strategies to navigate these challenges. The process requires each partner to introspect, identify their triggers and vulnerabilities, and communicate these openly. The resulting framework is not a constraint but a liberation, a set of principles that empower both partners to approach sensitive topics confidently and respectfully. It transforms the minefield of difficult conversations into a garden of growth, where honesty is cultivated with care and nurtured by mutual respect.

The creation of safe spaces for sharing, both physical and emotional, is integral to the practice of honesty. These sanctuaries, free from judgment and filled with understanding, offer partners the assurance they need to reveal their innermost thoughts and feelings. The physical dimension of this space might be a particular room or setting that inspires a sense of peace and privacy, while the emotional dimension is fostered through a consistent demonstration of empathy and support. It is in these havens that vulnerability is not just safe but sacred, where the seeds of truth can be sown with the certainty that they will be met with compassion. The ongoing nurturing of these spaces reflects the couple's dedication to fostering an environment where honesty can thrive. This process requires vigilance and commitment, as well as a continual effort to ensure that these sanctuaries remain protected from the corrosive effects of complacency and neglect.

Regular honesty check-ins emphasize the dynamic nature of relationships, acknowledging that trust and honesty are constantly evolving. These scheduled sessions are opportunities for renewal and reaffirmation; moments set aside to reflect on the state of the relationship's honesty. They serve as a barometer, measuring the pressures and temperatures within the partnership, identifying areas of strength, and highlighting those needing attention. In these discussions, partners engage in a review of their interactions and a renewal of their commitment to transparency and trust. This practice underscores the belief that honesty is an active endeavor, a dynamic relationship element that requires nurturing and attention. These check-ins, marked on the calendar with the same importance as anniversaries and birthdays, become rituals of connection, reinforcing the foundation upon which the relationship stands.

In the realm of love and commitment, where the veil between the self and the other becomes permeable, the dialogue on honesty is both a challenge and a gift. It demands the courage to speak the truth and the grace to receive others with openness and empathy. The establishment of ground rules for honesty, the creation of safe spaces for sharing, and the institution of regular check-ins are not mere strategies but acts of love, a testament to the couple's commitment to fostering a relationship where trust is not just a principle but a lived reality. In this endeavor, the nuances of communication, the subtleties of understanding, and the depths of empathy are explored, crafting a partnership where honesty thrives, not as an obligation but as a shared value, a beacon guiding the relationship through the complexities of human connection.

Sharing Secrets: Deepening Emotional Intimacy

In the intricate weave of emotional intimacy that binds partners, the sharing of secrets stands as a pivotal thread, a conduit through which the deepest layers of trust are tested and fortified. This delicate act requires a space where the heart's vault can be unlocked, revealing its contents not to the harsh glare of judgment but to the soft light of understanding and acceptance. The process of exchanging these hidden truths, each a fragment of the self that is kept away from the world's eyes, becomes a ritual of connection, a mutual unveiling that bridges souls.

Structured and meticulously designed activities support this delicate exchange, confidently guiding partners through the complexities of vulnerability. These activities, ranging from guided conversations under the night sky to written exchanges where words flow freely without the pressure of immediate response, are designed to facilitate the sharing of secrets and ensure that the process enriches rather than over-whelms. In these moments, sharing becomes more than just an exchange of information; it transforms into a sacred communion, reflecting the safety and sanctity of the bond.

The emphasis on creating a safe space for this exchange must be balanced. This sanctuary, free from the threat of judgment or negativity, is essential for the heart to open fully and for the guarded secrets to be shared. Establishing this haven requires an explicit agreement that the truths shared will be met with empathy, held in confidence, and honored with respect. Within this safe space, vulnerabilities can be exposed without fear, and sharing secrets becomes an act of trust, a leap into the unknown with the assurance of a soft landing.

The process of sharing secrets rests on the twin pillars of confidentiality and respect for boundaries. The act of entrusting another with a piece of one's hidden self is a gesture of immense faith, a belief in the other's capacity to hold this gift with care. Thus, the commitment to confiden-tiality becomes a sacred duty, a vow that the secrets shared will remain within the heart of the relationship, shielded from the outside world. Likewise, the respect for boundaries ensures that this exchange is not an imposition but a gift freely given and received, a delicate dance of give-and-take that respects each partner's comfort and readiness limits.

Sharing secrets, therefore, is a powerful tool for deepening emotional intimacy. It is a deliberate step into vulnerability that strengthens the fabric of trust. While fraught with the potential for discomfort, it holds the promise of unparalleled connection, a bond forged in the trial of openness. It acknowledges that the strength of a relationship lies not in the absence of secrets but in the capacity to share them, to see and be seen in the totality of one's being.

These structured activities, from spoken words to written confessions, serve as a means for deeper connection. They allow partners to explore the landscapes of their inner worlds together. They are invitations to journey beyond the surface, to venture into the realms of fear, hope, and aspiration that lie beneath. In this exploration, partners discover not only each other but themselves, unearthing long-buried truths and seeing their reflections in the mirror of the other's under-standing.

This journey into the heart's hidden chambers requires courage and a willingness to traverse the shadows in search of light. It demands a mutual commitment to empathy, confi-dentiality, and respect, a shared dedication to creating a space where the soul can speak without fear. In this space, secrets become not barriers to intimacy but bridges that lead to a deeper understanding and connection.

Sharing secrets is a vital aspect of a relationship, a component that, when approached with care, deepens the connection between partners. It embodies the trust that forms the foundation of emotional intimacy, a trust that is both fragile and resilient, capable of withstanding challenges and emerging stronger. In this shared vulnerability, partners find not weakness but strength, not isolation but connection, a deepening of the bond that sustains them through the uncertainties of life.

Within the experience of love and connection, where the heart seeks comfort and adventure, sharing secrets offers a path to both. It is a journey marked by the willingness to reveal and to receive, to accept and to understand. Through this mutual unveiling, partners build a bond of intimacy that is both gentle and strong, showcasing the enduring power of trust and the transformative potential of openness. In this sacred exchange, the relationship finds its most profound expression, a harmony of souls that resonates with the truth of shared secrets and the beauty of unconditional acceptance.

Technology Detox: Reconnecting Offline

As screens increasingly dominate our lives and threaten authentic human connection, intentionally stepping away from digital devices becomes a significant gesture toward nurturing the bond that thrives in the physical world. A technology detox, thus, emerges not as an escape but as a deliberate return to the essence of companionship, where the immediacy of face-to-face interaction reclaims its rightful place at the heart of the relationship. This withdrawal from the digital into the physical is an invitation to rediscover the nuances of conversation, the subtleties of expression, and the richness of shared silence, elements often obscured by the barrage of notifications and the allure of endless content.

The start of this detox relies on the mutual recognition of its necessity, a shared understanding that the constant presence of technology compromises the relationship. This acknowledgment leads to a plan for disengaging from the digital world and reengaging with each other. The parameters of this plan are defined by the unique dynamics of the relationship and tailored to accommodate the rhythms of daily life while challenging the status quo of constant connectivity. It might specify hours of intermission from devices or designate entire days as digital-free, creating pockets of presence amid the desert of distraction.

The activities chosen for these detox periods are designed to fill the void left by technology with enriching and fulfilling experiences. Outdoor adventures beckon with the promise of nature's unfiltered beauty, inviting couples to immerse themselves in settings where the only likes and shares come from the exchange of awed glances and whispered appreciations of the world around them. The preparation of meals, from the selection of ingredients to the savoring of the finished dish, becomes an act of collaborative creation, a dance of flavors and aromas that celebrates the joy of shared endeavors. These simple yet profound activities serve as reminders of the pleasures to be found in direct engagement with the world and each other, pleasures often overlooked in the rush to document rather than experience.

The benefits of withdrawing from the digital world into direct interaction are manifold. Intimacy finds new avenues of expression in the undivided attention partners offer each other, in the conversations that flow unhindered by the ping of incoming messages, and in the rediscovery of each other's quirks and traits outside the curated portrayals of social media. Presence, the most elusive of states in an age of multitasking, becomes the default, transforming shared moments into treasures of connection and understanding. This detox is not a negation of technology's value but an affirmation of the relationship's importance, a recalibration of priorities that places the partnership at the center, surrounded but not overshadowed by the digital world.

As this chapter on deliberate disconnection draws to a close, it leaves behind the echo of its central tenets: the recognition of technology's impact on the fabric of relationships, the intentional creation of spaces free from digital intrusion, and the cultivation of activities that foster direct engagement and presence. These principles, woven into the daily rhythm of the partnership, serve as a counterbalance to the digital age's demands, a reminder of the enduring value of face-to-face connection. In pursuing a bond that thrives in the real world, the technology detox acts not as an end goal but as a means to deepen intimacy and presence in an increasingly connected world.

As we turn the page from this exploration of reconnection through disconnection, we carry forward the insights gleaned from stepping back into the physical realm, embracing the richness of experience that awaits beyond the screen. This journey through the deliberate cultivation of presence and intimacy paves the way for the chapters to come, each exploring new dimensions of nurturing the bond at the heart of the relationship.

NINE

Navigating The Waters of Digital Presence

With the digital age in full swing, the ever-present nature of digital footprints and the shadows they cast over relationships become a topic that demands attention. From the early days of email and instant messaging to the current era of social media and mobile apps, technology's role in shaping modern relationships has evolved with an undeniable force. As much as technology has bridged gaps and forged connections, it has also introduced layers of complexity to relationships, requiring careful attention to maintain their integrity.

The Dual-edged Sword of Social Media

The advent of social media brought with it a revolution in the way individuals connect, communicate, and perceive one another. Its capacity to unite people is rivaled only by its potential to pull them apart. In the context of a relationship, social media presents a double-edged sword, offering a platform for connection and expression while simultaneously posing challenges that may lead to friction. The key to harnessing its benefits while sidestepping its pitfalls lies in a concerted effort to establish boundaries that both partners can agree upon, respect, and uphold.

Establishing Boundaries: A Path to Harmony

Delineating boundaries—what is shared and what remains private—is the first step toward navigating the digital terrain together. Consider, for instance, a couple that decides that photographs of their relationship's private moments will remain just that—private—and will not be uploaded without mutual consent. Setting this boundary is a foundational step that fosters a climate of mutual respect and understanding.

The Digital Etiquette: A Guide to Coexistence

As much as personal spaces demand respect, so does the digital realm. The ability to recognize and respect the boundary between what is personal and what is shareable marks a significant stride toward fostering mutual trust. The digital landscape, with its endless streams and feeds, calls for a form of digital etiquette—a set of shared understandings that guide interactions in a world of shared experiences.

Reflections on Digital Footprints: A Path Less Taken

Addressing the challenges posed by social media requires a conscious effort to engage in reflective practices that examine personal and shared digital behaviors. This could involve periodically reviewing the content both partners share online, discussing how it reflects their shared values, and exploring opportunities to enrich their digital presence with content that enhances their relationship. These reflective practices encourage partners not only to be mindful of the content they share but also to be attentive to the digital footprints they leave behind.

Charting a Course: Navigating the Digital Seas Together

Much like the ocean, the digital realm is vast and filled with opportunities and challenges. Establishing a shared presence online—such as a joint blog or social media account dedicated to documenting shared experiences—offers couples a way to weave their online narratives. This shared space becomes a platform for collective expression, a place where they can create and share content that reflects their visions and values.

Interactive Element: Navigating Social Media Together - A Survey

This interactive element invites partners to step back and assess their digital habits and interactions. The survey includes questions on topics such as individual online behaviors, feelings toward each other's digital presence, and areas where communication can improve. This interactive experience encourages dialogue and provides a structured framework for partners to explore their digital interactions and identify areas where adjustments may be needed.

The Road Ahead: A Shared Journey

With all its complexities, the digital world offers a new frontier for exploration—a place where love, respect, and mutual understanding can be fostered. Though fraught with challenges, the journey through this digital landscape offers opportunities for growth and connection. The key to this journey is a mutual commitment to understanding, respecting, and accommodating each other's needs and preferences. Through this commitment, couples can chart a course that honors both individual identities and shared experiences, forging a meaningful and enduring path.

Exploring the digital world together requires a deliberate and thoughtful approach, one that acknowledges the complexities of online interactions while celebrating the opportunities for connection these digital platforms offer. As partners journey through this digital space, they encounter challenges and opportunities to grow and learn together. This online environment, with its potential for shared experiences and personal expression, reflects the strength and resilience of relationships in today's tech-driven society.

Long-Distance Love: Keeping Connected

Distance in love poses a formidable challenge, testing resilience and measuring devotion. But this distance, however daunting, is not impossible, thanks in part to the tools of the digital age that facilitate intimacy and connection across miles. A long-distance relationship, filled with feelings of longing and affection, gains strength from technology, which acts as a bridge that unites partners despite physical separation.

The core element of maintaining the liveliness of a relationship marred by distance is the commitment to regular, meaningful communication. Video calls, which transcend the limitations of traditional phone conversations, offer a window into the lives of partners separated by geography. This visual connection, a lifeline in the sea of separation, enables the sharing of expressions, the warmth of smiles, and the comfort of presence, even in a digital form. Whether daily check-ins or weekly deep dives, these calls become a ritual of connection, reaffirming the bond that distance seeks to stretch thin.

The digital realm brims with countless other opportunities for shared experiences. Online games, ranging from the simplicity of board game adaptations to the complexity of virtual worlds, become settings for companionship, laughter, and teamwork. These games, more than mere pastimes, are exercises in collaboration and support, a dance of minds that mirrors the partnership's dynamics. Similarly, digital dates, where couples synchronize their screens to watch a movie, cook a meal, or explore virtual galleries together, simulate the shared experiences that physical proximity affords. These meticulously planned, and eagerly anticipated activities are oases in the desert of distance; they are moments when miles of separation seem to vanish.

Partners' creativity in long-distance relationships often flourishes in the face of separation, finding expression in gestures that bridge the gap between the tangible and the virtual. Digital gifts, whether subscriptions to streaming services, online courses, or curated playlists, carry the weight of thoughtfulness and care. These tokens of affection are reminders of the partner's presence in daily life, a nudge in the side that says, "You are on my mind." The act of sending a digital gift, though devoid of physical exchange, is rich with symbolism, a testament to the effort and intention invested in keeping the spark alive.

Amid the bounty of tools, couples navigating long-distance relationships confront challenges that demand attention and strategy. The specter of miscommunication, exacerbated by the absence of non-verbal cues and the coldness of text, is a frequent visitor to conversations held across screens. Addressing this challenge requires a deliberate emphasis on clarity and openness, an agreement to err on the side of over-communication rather than risk the chasm of misunderstanding. This approach, coupled with the understanding that words, without physical cues, carry the burden of conveying tone, intention, and emotion, guides partners toward a communication style marked by patience and empathy.

The natural cycle of daily responsibilities and distractions often presents another hurdle for long-distance couples. Finding windows of time that align across time zones, work schedules, and social commitments is like solving a puzzle, a test of flexibility and compromise. The strategy to overcome this challenge hinges on prioritizing the relationship and marking time for each other as one would for any indispensable aspect of life. This prioritization, a conscious choice to keep the relationship at the forefront, ensures that the threads of connection, though stretched, remain strong and resilient.

In long-distance relationships, technology emerges not just as a tool but as a lifeline, helping to overcome the physical barriers that separation imposes. It provides a space for creativity, a platform for shared experiences, and enables the continuous exchange of affection and support. The strategies couples use to leverage these digital resources reflect their commitment to nurturing their bond and ensuring that distance does not hinder intimacy and connection.

The journey through a long-distance relationship, fortified by the thoughtful use of technology, showcases the enduring power of love. It tells a story of resilience, where couples discover ways to connect, share, and grow despite the miles between them. In this endeavor, technology serves as a bridge, facilitating the love that distance attempts to test but ultimately helps to strengthen.

Modern Parenting: Sharing the Load

As family life becomes increasingly intertwined with digital elements, parenting is undergoing a significant transformation. Raising children is as demanding as it is rewarding, often requiring a delicate balance to manage effectively. Technology emerges as an ally in this context, offering tools and platforms designed to streamline the complexities of modern parenting. Through apps and online resources, partners can divide the labor of parenting more evenly, reducing stress and enhancing the teamwork that forms the backbone of a healthy family dynamic.

The integration of technology into the daily rituals of family life begins with exploring apps and online tools designed for managing schedules, chores, and activities. With their customizable features and user-friendly interfaces, these digital assistants serve as central hubs for coordinating the numerous tasks that parenting demands. From tracking doctor's appointments to organizing playdates and extracurricular activities, these platforms offer a solution to the once-daunting task of keeping informed of family commitments. Sharing access to these tools allows both partners to contribute to planning and organization, ensuring that the responsibility does not fall disproportionately on one individual. This collaborative approach fosters a sense of unity and partnership, reinforcing the foundation for effective co-parenting.

The digital age also has ushered in unprecedented access to parenting insights and resources. Online forums, blogs, and social media groups provide a vast reservoir of knowledge and experiences parents from diverse backgrounds share. These platforms offer advice and solace in the shared challenges of parenting, forging connections between individuals who, though separated by distance, are united in their roles as caregivers. The ability to tap into this collective wisdom allows partners to explore new strategies for addressing the challenges they face, from navigating the complexities of child development to managing behavioral issues. The exchange of ideas and support through these digital channels illuminates the path for parents seeking guidance, offering fresh perspectives and innovative solutions.

The pivotal role of technology in facilitating communication between partners cannot be understated. With the advent of shared digital calendars and messaging apps, the coordination of parenting duties has become a seamless affair. These tools allow for real-time updates and reminders, ensuring that both partners are informed and engaged in the logistics of family life. The ability to communicate efficiently reduces the potential for oversight and miscommunication, hallmarks of stress in the parenting journey. Through these platforms, the small details of family logistics are negotiated and managed, allowing parents to focus on the more rewarding aspects of their roles.

The fair distribution of parenting responsibilities, now more achievable with the help of technology, requires a conscious effort to utilize these tools effectively. Tips for making the most of digital resources include setting clear expectations for their use, customizing features to fit the family's unique needs, and regularly reviewing and adjusting schedules and plans as necessary. Implementing these strategies ensures that technology facilitates harmony and efficiency in family life.

In modern parenting, technology serves as both thread and needle, intricately linking the responsibilities and joys of raising children. It creates a bridge over the potential gaps in miscommunication and fairness, guiding partners toward a partnership that is both supportive and balanced. By thoughtfully using digital tools, parents can tackle the challenges of their roles with grace, ensuring that the journey of family life is one marked by collaboration and mutual support.

Balancing Work and Love in the Digital Age

As the digital world profoundly redefines professional life, the line between work and leisure has grown increasingly vague, making it more essential than ever to thoughtfully and deliberately separate work from love. The maze of remote work and digital interference presents a unique set of challenges, yet within its confines lie opportunities for couples to develop strategies that nurture their bond.

Establishing clear distinctions between periods allocated for professional duties and those reserved for personal interaction is pivotal. This endeavor is similar to cartography, wherein couples chart a map that honors the sanctity of shared time amid the fluidity of digital work schedules. Consider, for instance, the ritual of commencing each day with a shared intention-setting session, a brief interlude when partners articulate their aspirations for the day, both work-related and personal. Such practices act not only as anchors but also as reminders of the importance of their relationship in the daily swirl of obligations.

Furthermore, despite its challenges, the digital era offers tools that help balance work commitments with personal life. Work arrangements, now untethered from the physicality of office spaces, offer a flexibility that can yield pockets of quality time. Couples who synchronize their work blocks and breaks allow moments of connection to blossom amid professional endeavors. Shared digital calendars become a logistical tool and a canvas to paint a balanced coexistence of work and love.

Establishing physical and digital work zones is critical for remote work, where the home doubles as an office. Designating specific areas for professional activities creates a sanctuary for focus, a physical boundary that, once crossed, signals a return to personal life. The meticulous orchestration of these spaces, coupled with the use of digital tools to limit work-related notifications beyond designated hours, defends against the intrusion of professional obligations into personal time.

Practical guidance for couples wandering the complexities of digital work arrangements emphasizes the cultivation of rituals that foster connectivity. Instituting a daily digital detox, a period when devices are set aside in favor of face-to-face interaction, can counterbalance the day's digital immersion. This practice, simple in its essence but profound in its impact, shifts the focus from screens to the shared physicality of presence. In addition, the deliberate engagement in activities absent of digital interference—whether a walk in nature, a shared culinary adventure, or the pursuit of a mutual hobby

—reaffirms the value of direct experience, a reminder of the texture and depth that tactile experiences add to a relationship.

Combining work and love in the digital age demands mindfulness and creativity. The challenges are significant but not insurmountable, and the strategies for addressing them testify to the resilience and adaptability of couples committed to nurturing their bond. The endeavor to balance the scales between professional obligations and the nourishment of personal connections is an ongoing process that requires constant negotiation and recalibration. Yet, the potential for growth lies within this process, for in seeking equilibrium, couples discover new dimensions of their relationship, new strengths, and new avenues for connection.

The landscape of love and work in the digital age is one of contrasts—of flexibility and intrusion, of opportunities and challenges—that demands guidance with both intention and grace. While fraught with potential pitfalls, this journey is filled with avenues for deepening connections. In this endeavor, strategies are established, and boundaries are set that serve as guideposts, illuminating a path where the harmony of professional and personal life is not just a distant ideal but an attainable reality. Through the astute management of digital demands and the deliberate cultivation of shared experiences, couples can craft a thriving relationship that transcends the challenges of remote work and digital distractions.

Customizable Relationship Apps and Tools

The essence of digital applications and tools designed to address relationship dynamics lies in their ability to be tailored to the specific contours of each relationship, offering a personalized approach to nurturing the bond between partners.

The spectrum of available apps serves a dual purpose: facilitating the logistics of shared lives while simultaneously offering avenues for emotional and romantic enrichment. For instance, apps that track significant dates and anniversaries function as more than mere reminders; they are a call for celebration, a nudge toward recognizing the milestones of a partnership. Similarly, applications designed to schedule date nights or propose activities based on shared interests act as catalysts for quality time, transforming the often-daunting task of planning into a seamless, enjoyable process.

The selection of the right digital tools is critical. It requires understanding each partner's unique needs and preferences, a commitment to exploring the functionalities of different apps, and a willingness to experiment with options. The criteria for this selection process are as varied as the apps themselves, encompassing factors such as user interface, privacy settings, customization options, and the ability to sync across devices. The objective is to identify applications that resonate with the couple's lifestyle, enhance their relationship by fostering communication, streamline the organization of shared responsibilities, and create opportunities for spontaneous romantic gestures.

Utilizing these apps and tools transcends mere convenience; it is an exercise in intentionality. By actively engaging with these digital resources, couples reaffirm their commitment to their relationship. For example, using an app to plan surprise date nights introduces an element of unpredictability and excitement, rekindling the sense of adventure that often fades into the routine of daily life. Likewise, leveraging platforms that offer guided conversations or relationship-building activities encourages partners to explore new dimensions of their connection, fostering a deeper understanding and appreciation for one another.

There are multiple ways to explore this digital terrain. Initially, partners should engage in open discussions about the use of technology in their relationship and establish a shared vision for how these tools can enhance their bond. Subsequently, a period of exploration and experimentation with different apps can help identify those that best align with this vision. Finally, setting regular intervals to review and assess the impact of these tools on the relationship ensures that they continue to serve their intended purpose.

As the virtual and tangible boundaries continue to blur, customizable apps and tools that foster relationship growth, communication, and intimacy serve as a bridge between the digital and the physical. They embody the potential for technology not just to occupy space within a relationship but to enrich it, not just to facilitate the logistics of togetherness but to enhance the experience of connection.

Exploring these digital offerings is a voyage into the heart of the relationship. It is an opportunity to reaffirm priorities, rediscover joys, and deepen the bond that unites partners. In this context, technology transcends its role as a tool and becomes a companion on the path to a more fulfilling partnership.

As we conclude this exploration, we are reminded of the transformative potential of thoughtfully integrating technology into our relationships. The apps and tools we have at our disposal serve as vessels for growth, communication, and intimacy; they offer new avenues for connection in an increasingly digital world. Though this chapter ventures into the digital realm, it ultimately highlights the enduring power of love and partnership, celebrating the ways in which technology can strengthen the bonds that unite us.

TEN

Bridging Hearts with Digital Threads

I n an era where silence often speaks louder than words, the hum of technology offers a symphony of solutions for those willing to listen. The tap of a keyboard can send a heart fluttering, and the ping of a notification can bridge miles of longing. Technology that once was deemed a distraction now emerges as a lifeline for couples navigating the complexities of connection across the voids of circumstance.

Overcoming Communication Barriers with Tech

Breaking Down Walls, Byte by Byte

Within the world of human connection, instances of misunderstanding can easily disrupt even the most joyful relationships. Yet, in this digital age, technology plays a significant role in untangling miscommunications with the precision of instant messaging, the clarity offered by translation apps, and the inclusivity provided by accessibility features. Imagine a Saturday morning when a couple, separated by continents and time zones, finds comfort in the shared silence of a video call, their smiles bridging the distance and transcending the need for words.

Case Studies: Technology as the Great Communicator

Reflecting on real-world scenarios, we find technology playing the role of mediator in relationships strained by distance and differing schedules. A couple running on opposite clocks who previously struggled to align their lives now find rhythm through shared online calendars and synchronized digital reminders. Here, technology acts not as a barrier but as a bridge, turning missed connections into moments of anticipation for shared digital experiences.

Embracing Diversity Through Digital Dialogue

The role of technology in facilitating communication extends its hand generously to couples wrestling with the challenges of disabilities. Accessibility features in communication apps offer a voice to those for whom speaking was a mountain too steep to climb. Text-to-speech functions and real-time sign language interpretation services weave a web of understanding, turning frustrations into opportunities for deeper empathy.

Insights from the Digital Frontier

By examining these examples of digital success, we uncover strategies enriched by technology. Couples find that setting specific times for digital get-togethers creates a sanctuary of connection amid the chaos of daily life. Apps designed for relationship enrichment offer prompts for discussions that might otherwise remain buried under the cloak of routine, allowing couples to explore the depths of their relationship with the tap of a screen.

Interactive Element: Navigating Communication Apps

A curated list of communication apps and tools becomes a treasure trove for couples eager to deepen their dialogue. Accompanied by a quiz that assesses communication styles and preferences, this resource offers personalized app recommendations. From apps that translate love languages into actionable tasks to those that schedule heart-to-heart conversations, technology tailors itself to the heart's needs.

In a landscape where digital and emotional realms intertwine, technology shines as a beacon for couples exploring the seas of communication. It offers solutions and pathways to understanding, proving that even in silence, connection thrives. Through the lens of technology, we see a world drawn closer by digital communication, fostering connections filled with understanding, empathy, and love.

Intimacy Reimagined: How Couples Rediscovered Their Spark

Amid the delicate interplay of relationships, the ember of romance, while resilient, requires intentional nurturing to transform into a steady flame. Reviving this spark amidst the chaos of daily obligations showcases the enduring power of love and the creative spirit of committed partners. Through innovative approaches to reignite romance, change routines, and embrace shared experiences, couples embark on a journey toward a rejuvenated bond filled with passion and connection.

Revitalizing Romance

In the realm of love, the unexpected gesture, the surprise that breaks the monotony of the everyday, can act as a spark for renewed passion. Stories abound of partners orchestrating elaborate surprises, from clandestine getaways to the recreation of first dates, each act infused with intention and desire. These stories illustrate the careful planning of transforming an ordinary Tuesday into a romantic escape. A path of rose petals leads to a candlelit setting, creating an intimate atmosphere where the world outside fades away, allowing couples to focus solely on each other.

The power of the written word, too, finds its place in the arsenal of romantic rekindling. Love letters, penned with the ink of raw emotion, bridge the gap between hearts, carrying whispers of affection and promises of perpetual devotion. These letters, often shared in moments carved out of the rush of life, serve as tangible reminders of the depth of the bond, a physical manifestation of love that endures the test of time and circumstance.

Deepening Emotional Connection

The journey toward deepening emotional intimacy navigates the terrain of vulnerability, where open hearts converge in a space of mutual understanding. Practices such as "The Mirror Exercise," where partners hold a gaze, undistracted, sharing unspoken truths through the windows of the soul, foster a profound connection. This silent dialogue, stripped of pretense, invites authenticity, revealing fears, dreams, and the raw essence of each individual.

Conversations also deepen, moving beyond the superficial to explore hopes, insecurities, and the reflective ideas that occupy the mind. These dialogues, often initiated through prompts designed to peel back the layers of the psyche, encourage a nakedness of the soul, where secrets and dreams are shared with the trust that they will be cradled with care and empathy.

Physical Connection Renewed

Rediscovering physical intimacy in its many forms acts as a bridge to deeper closeness, reinforcing a bond that goes beyond the physical. Couples explore new dimensions of touch, from the feather-light caress tracing the contours of a face to the firm grip of hands intertwined, each contact a word in the language of love. Exploring sensory experiences, such as blindfolded taste tests or the exchange of massages, heightens awareness, drawing partners into a dance of sensation and discovery.

Challenges related to intimacy, once barriers, transform into opportunities for growth and exploration. Through open discussions and the willingness to experiment, couples explore the nuances of physical connection, discovering new sources of pleasure and reaffirming their attraction and desire for one another.

Shared Adventures

Embarking on shared adventures sparks excitement and novelty in the relationship. These ventures, ranging from the thrill of skydiving to the serenity of sunrise hikes, embody the essence of partnership—a mutual reliance on one another in the face of the unknown. The planning and anticipation involved in these adventures generate excitement, where the journey is just as important as the destination.

Adventures don't always have to be extreme; trying out new hobbies or classes together offers a space for shared growth and the joy of learning alongside one another. Discovering shared passions or appreciating each other's interests builds a foundation of respect and admiration, reinforcing the partnership.

The essence of romance, intimacy, and shared experiences, once diminished by time and the monotony of daily life, is renewed by those dedicated to nurturing love. Through deliberate actions, surprises, and embracing vulnerability and adventure, couples reforge their bonds, discovering new depths of love and connection in each other. This journey of rediscovery, marked by creativity and a willingness to explore the uncharted territories of each other's hearts, rekindles the spark of romance, ensuring that the flame of love burns brighter, illuminating the path forward together.

Building Trust in the Age of Digital Transparency

In today's complex world of modern love, the balance between digital transparency and privacy poses significant challenges to trust. The online space, holding our deepest secrets and casual thoughts, stands at the crossroads of intimacy and independence. It requires couples to handle this delicate balance with care, respecting both their connection and personal boundaries. The dance between openness and individuality in this digital age requires not just steps but a choreography that honors the sanctity of both shared and solitary spaces.

In this intricate ballet, social media platforms play a pivotal role, serving as stages upon which our lives unfold. The decision to share or withhold parts of our digital selves becomes a nuanced negotiation within relationships, a delicate balance between the desire for connection and the need for personal territory. Couples find themselves at the negotiating table, drafting unwritten agreements that delineate the boundaries of their digital coexistence. These agreements, fluid, and ever-evolving, reflect the dynamic nature of relationships, adapting to the rhythms of life's changes and technological advances.

The sharing of devices, a commonplace practice in the intimacy of shared lives, brings questions of access and autonomy to the front. Here, trust manifests in the unspoken agreements that govern the use of shared technology. An unlocked phone on the kitchen counter becomes a testament to trust, a symbol of openness that coexists with the silent acknowledgment of each partner's right to privacy. This equilibrium, carefully maintained, relies on the mutual understanding that access does not equate to surveillance and that the shared use of technology is a privilege born of trust, not a tool for monitoring.

Online histories, those digital footprints left in the sand of our internet visits, offer a window into the private worlds of curiosity, fear, and desire that shape us. For couples, the choice to share these histories—or not—is symbolic of the trust that underpins their relationship. It is an acknowledgment that while our digital explorations are part of who we are, they do not define the entirety of ourselves or our relationship. The respect for this aspect of digital privacy underscores a deeper trust, one that understands the importance of individual exploration within the context of a committed partnership.

Case studies drawn from the heart of the digital age illustrate the various ways couples navigate these challenges. One narrative tells of partners who, finding themselves at odds over the visibility of their online interactions, embark on a dialogue that culminates in creating a shared digital philosophy. This philosophy, a beacon guiding their online engagement, underscores the importance of mutual respect for privacy while fostering a culture of openness and honesty.

One account describes the journey of a couple who, by using app-controlled permissions, find a balance that allows them to share aspects of their digital lives while respecting personal boundaries. These stories, reflective of the broader experience of love in the digital age, highlight couples' adaptive strategies to cultivate trust in the shadow of digital transparency.

Strategies for approaching this complex landscape emphasize the importance of open dialogue and mutual agreement. They suggest regular check-ins, where couples can reflect on their digital engagement and renegotiate boundaries as necessary. These discussions, far from signifying distrust, are markers of a healthy relationship that recognizes the evolving nature of both technology and human connection. Establishing digital boundaries agreed upon by both partners serves as a foundation for this dialogue, providing a framework within which trust can flourish.

To cultivate trust in the digital realm, couples are encouraged to approach their online engagement with intentionality and transparency. This means making conscious choices about what to share, with whom, and when, decisions that are informed by a shared understanding of each partner's comfort levels and privacy needs. Adopting digital practices that prioritize transparency, such as sharing passwords or social media profiles, is balanced by acknowledging each person's need for a private digital space. This balance, carefully maintained, ensures that the digital realm becomes a space of connection rather than contention.

As couples face the challenges of digital transparency, they must explore unfamiliar waters where technology intersects with the intricacies of human emotion. Building trust in this environment becomes a collaborative effort, requiring both partners to proceed with care and communicate clearly. As they move forward, guided by the principles of openness and respect, they create a path that honors their individual journeys and their shared destination.

Creative Conflict Resolution with Virtual Mediation

Within the complexities of relationships, where two lives merge to create a beautiful yet challenging harmony, conflicts can sometimes arise, disrupting the balance partners have carefully built so diligently together. This disruption, while unsettling, is not beyond repair; it calls for a skilled conductor to restore the symphony of mutual understanding and respect. This is where virtual mediation and online counseling services come into play—a modern guide experienced in addressing the nuances of conflict, working to achieve resolutions that resonate with both partners.

The digital revolution has unfurled a canvas upon which conflicts, once deemed impossible by distance or circumstance, can now be addressed with an expertise that transcends geographical limitations. Virtual mediation emerges as a beacon for couples trapped in the agony of disagreement, offering a platform where voices are heard, emotions are acknowledged, and resolutions are crafted with the guidance of seasoned professionals. The virtual space becomes a sanctuary, a neutral space where the challenges of conflict are carefully untangled by a skilled mediator, blending compromise and understanding to strengthen the bond of the relationship.

In this space, stories of transformation flourish—tales of couples who, facing the brink of conflict, found comfort and resolution through the guidance of virtual mediators. Consider the tale of a couple, their harmony disrupted by the relentless pace of modern life, who discovered a haven for their grievances to be aired without fear of judgment in the virtual mediation space. Guided by a mediator whose influence, though digital, was still impactful, they worked through the entanglement of misunderstandings to a place of mutual respect and renewed commitment. Another account details partners divided by ideological differences, exacerbated by the echo chambers of social media, who sought the guidance of an online therapist to bridge the gap between them. Through sessions that spanned keyboards and screens, they embarked on a journey of introspection and empathy, each step guided by insights illuminating the path to a deeper, more resilient union.

The advantages of seeking professional guidance in the virtual realm are countless, illuminated by its convenience and comfort. For those tangled in the web of busy schedules or constrained by the absence of local resources, online platforms offer a lifeline—a bridge to expertise and support that might otherwise remain beyond reach. The privacy afforded by virtual sessions, where the sanctity of personal space is preserved, fosters a sense of security, encouraging openness and vulnerability. Furthermore, the flexibility inherent in digital services allows for customization that caters to each relationship's unique rhythm and needs, ensuring that the crafted solution is as distinct as the melody of their love.

Navigating the selection and engagement with virtual mediation and counseling services necessitates discernment—a careful consideration of credentials, methodologies, and reviews that attest to the success and values of the provider. Partners are encouraged to engage in preliminary dialogues with potential mediators or counselors, which establishes rapport and offers insights into the compatibility of their approaches with the couple's expectations. The maximization of these services hinges upon clear communication of goals, an openness to the process, and a commitment to applying the insights and strategies gathered from sessions to the daily cadence of their relationship.

In this endeavor, the role of technology extends beyond that of a basic channel for conversation; it becomes an architect of solutions, a builder of bridges over the rivers of discord that occasionally traverse the landscape of love. The choice to engage with virtual mediation and counseling services is a testament to the resilience of relationships in the face of challenges—a declaration that even amid conflict, the pursuit of harmony, understanding, and growth remains a priority. Through the guidance of virtual mediators and counselors, couples are afforded not just resolutions to their disputes but also tools and strategies to fortify their bond against the turmoil of future disagreements.

In the grand composition of a relationship, where each note contributes to the melody of shared existence, the challenges faced serve as invitations to refine the harmony that connects partners. Virtual mediation and online counseling services stand as allies in this continuous process of tuning and retuning, ensuring that the music of love, with all its complexities and nuances, continues to evolve, resonate, and inspire.

Technology-Enhanced Date Nights and Quality Time

In the vast expanse of the digital age, where the soft glow of screens illuminates hidden corners of existence, technology emerges not as a mere backdrop but as a vibrant canvas for painting moments of connection between couples. The intricate dance of date nights and quality time, traditionally anchored in the physical presence, now spins gracefully into the digital domain, offering novel experiences that enrich the fabric of relationships. This transition, seamless in its integration, redefines the parameters of shared experiences, weaving technology into the golden threads of intimacy and companionship.

In this realm where innovation meets affection, stories flourish of couples transforming ordinary evenings into digital adventures. Each tale reflects the endless creativity that technology inspires, showcasing how tools can enhance connection and make moments truly special. Imagine a couple, separated by miles yet connected by screens, who transcend the physical divide by embarking on a culinary journey together. Through video calls, they guide each other through the steps of crafting a dish, each ingredient a symbol of their shared life, each flavor a memory revisited. This culinary escapade, facilitated by technology, becomes more than a meal; it is a ritual of love, a reaffirmation of the bond that distance cannot dim.

The significance of carving out quality time in the relentless march of daily life cannot be overstated, for it is in these moments that the essence of a relationship breathes and flourishes. Technology offers a conduit for prioritizing these moments, transforming the mundane into the magical. Scheduling apps become the guardians of shared time, reminders that amid the noise of commitments, the symphony of love requires its own stage. Setting aside time for each other, marked digitally as sacred, reinforces the commitment to nurturing the relationship and ensuring that the digital world enhances rather than encroaches on the sanctum of shared existence.

Ideas for technology-enhanced date nights abound in each scenario, creating a palette of possibilities tailored to the interests and inclinations of each couple. For art enthusiasts, virtual tours of world-renowned museums offer an evening of cultural exploration, where discussions of art pieces spark dialogues about dreams, perceptions, and the beauty of human creativity. For those captivated by the stars, astronomy apps offer a gateway to the cosmos, transforming a quiet night under the sky into a journey across the universe. These apps bring constellations to life to tell tales of ancient myths, while the vastness of space reflects the depth of their connection.

Yet, integrating technology into quality time extends beyond the planning of elaborate date nights; it encompasses the small, everyday moments that knit the fabric of intimacy. A playlist shared between partners, with each song representing a chapter in their journey, becomes a digital diary of emotions, readily accessible with a simple tap. Text messages, brief yet brimming with affection, serve as bridges over the hours of separation, reminders that love whispers not just in grand gestures but in the quiet moments of everyday life.

As couples explore this digital space, they discover new avenues for connection and a deeper appreciation for the potential of technology to serve as a companion in their journey. The careful selection of apps and platforms, guided by the desire to enrich rather than dilute the essence of their relationship, becomes a creative endeavor, a shared project that reflects their values and dreams. In this exploration, couples discover that technology, often criticized as a source of isolation, can, in fact, be a vessel of unity, a tool that, when used with intention and care, brings hearts closer, overcoming the challenges of distance and time.

As we draw the curtains on this exploration of technology-enhanced date nights and quality time, we are reminded of the enduring power of connection in the tapestry of human relationships. The stories shared, the ideas explored, and the strategies outlined serve as beacons, illuminating the path for couples seeking to approach the digital age with grace and purpose. In this journey, technology reveals itself not as a rival to intimacy but as its ally, a medium through which love finds new expressions and shared moments acquire new depths. This chapter, a blend of digital and emotional experiences, encourages us to re-envision the role of technology in our lives, not as a barrier but as a bridge, leading us to a future where connections are not just maintained but enriched, where love, in all its forms, flourishes in the light of innovation.

Conclusion

As we reach the closing pages of our shared journey, I want to take a moment to celebrate you. It requires immense courage and commitment to embark on the path toward a healthier, more fulfilling marriage. Your dedication to seeking improvement and making lasting changes speaks volumes about the depth of your love and your willingness to invest in your partnership's future. This journey is one of bravery, love, and the pursuit of happiness, and you've shown remarkable resilience every step of the way.

Throughout this book, we've explored the fundamental pillars essential to nurturing a thriving relationship: effective communication, trust-building, deepening intimacy, conflict resolution, and personal and mutual growth. We've delved into the nuances of modern relationship dynamics, emphasizing the crucial role of tailored communication strategies. Customizing how we communicate allows us to meet our partners where they are, fostering understanding and resilience in our relationships.

Trust and intimacy, as we've discovered, are the bedrock of any strong bond. These elements extend beyond physical closeness; they embrace the emotional, intellectual, and shared experiences that enrich our lives. Moreover, we've seen the transformative power of conflict resolution—how viewing disagreements as opportunities for growth rather than as insurmountable obstacles can significantly enhance the dynamics of our relationships.

The journey doesn't end here. I encourage you to continue setting individual and collective goals, embracing growth as a continuous journey that keeps your relationship vibrant and fulfilling. Apply the actionable guidance, practical exercises, and innovative strategies provided within these pages. Start with small steps, celebrate your progress, and remember that patience and persistence are your allies.

In an age where technology often seems more like a wedge than a bridge, I urge you to see it as a tool for enhancing your connection. Experiment with apps and digital platforms that support your relationship goals, whether it's for communication, scheduling date nights, or embarking on new adventures together. Technology, when used thoughtfully, can deepen your intimacy and shared experiences.

Imagine a future where your relationship is marked by enduring happiness and fulfillment, a testament to the power of commitment, effective communication, and deepening trust and intimacy. This vision is within reach. As you apply the strategies we've discussed, remember that the journey of improvement is ongoing, filled with both challenges and triumphs.

I invite you to share your experiences and successes with me and your fellow readers. Your stories of growth and connection will inspire and foster a sense of community and support among all who embark on this path.

Let me leave you with a message of encouragement: You have the power to create a lasting, loving marriage. Challenges are part of the journey, but with perseverance and dedication, the rewards are profound. Remember, every couple's journey is unique—adapt the advice and strategies in this book to fit your specific circumstances and needs.

Thank you for allowing me to be a part of your journey toward a more fulfilling partnership. Here's to your continued happiness and growth together.

With warmth and support,

D.S. Loden

Keeping the Marriage Alive

Now that you have all the tools to achieve a healthy marriage, it's time to pay it forward and help other couples on their journey.

By sharing your honest opinion of 'The Practical Guide to a Healthy Marriage' on Amazon, you're not just leaving a review—you're guiding fellow couples to the resources they need to cultivate lasting happiness together. Your review could be the key that unlocks a healthier, happier marriage for someone else.

Thank you for your contribution. Every review keeps the flame of a healthy marriage burning bright, and you're playing a crucial role in spreading that warmth to others.

Leave a review here!

References

Lmft, M. H. (2024, April 22). *Active listening: a key to deeper intimacy and understanding in your relationship. Holding Hope Marriage and Family Therapy.* https://holdinghopemft.com/active-listening-a-key-to-deeper-intimacy-and-understanding-in-your-relationship/

From Esther Perel's blog - Six essential practices to improve listening skills in relationships. (n.d.). https://www.estherperel.com/blog/six-essential-practices-to-improve-listening-skills-in-relationships

BetterHelp Editorial Team. (2024, October 10). *How reading body language Can Improve your relationship | BetterHelp.* https://www.betterhelp.com/advice/body-language/how-reading-body-language-can-improve-your-relationship/

Ackerman, C. (2024, June 26). *21 Mindfulness Exercises & Activities for Adults (+ PDF). PositivePsychology.* Retrieved November 5, 2024, from https://positivepsychology.com/mindfulness-exercises-techniques-activities/

Zarch, Z. N., Marashi, S. M., & Raji, H. (2014, October 1). *The Relationship between Emotional Intelligence and Marital Satisfaction: 10-Year Outcome of Partners from Three Different Economic Levels.* https://www.ncbi.nlm.nih.gov/pmc/articles/PMC4361820/

MasterClass. (2022, June 6). *How to build emotional safety in a relationship - 2024.* https://www.masterclass.com/articles/emotional-safety

Pajer, N. (2021, May 12). *Navigating different communication styles in relationships. Shondaland.* https://www.shondaland.com/live/family/a36396758/navigating-different-communication-styles-in-relationships/

Kalie. (2024, March 15). *Why scheduling sex is one of the BEST things for a relationship. FULLforLife.* https://fullforlife.com/why-scheduling-sex-is-one-of-the-best-things-for-a-relationship/

Lcsw, J. L. (2024, April 21). *31 Fun Couples Therapy Exercises for bonding and communication. Counseling Palette.* https://www.thecounselingpalette.com/post/couples-therapy-exercises

How your brain responds to sex. (2020, February 5). [Video]. NBC News. https://www.nbcnews.com/better/lifestyle/how-build-emotional-intimacy-your-partner-starting-tonight-ncna1129846

Scharlop, M. (2024, February 21). *Benefits of hobbies for married couples.*

Plantation Relationship Counseling. https://plantationrelationshipcounsel ing.com/benefits-of-hobbies-for-married-couples/

BetterHelp Editorial Team. (2024a, October 9). Strengthen your relationship with 11 fun love apps for couples | BetterHelp. https://www.betterhelp.com/advice/ love/11-fun-love-apps-for-couples-that-could-improve-your-relationship/

Bethtbf. (2023, March 27). The dangers of social media on marriage and family. National University. https://www.nu.edu/blog/the-dangers-of-social-media-on-marriage-and-family/

Vr, Z. (2024, January 26). Best VR Games to Play with Your Partner - A Valentine's Day Adventure. ZyberVR. https://zybervr.com/blogs/news/best-vr-games-to-play-with-your-partner-a-valentines-day-adventure

Schumer, L., & Jenkins, C. (2024, February 28). 25 Fun Long-Distance Date ideas that go beyond FaceTime. Good Housekeeping. https://www.good housekeeping.com/life/relationships/a43095551/long-distance-date-ideas/

Hailey, L. (2023, December 11). 30 Best Trust-Building Exercises to Rebuild Relationships. Science of People. https://www.scienceofpeople.com/trust-building-exercises/

Savra, J. (n.d.). Why communication is important in a marriage | Jousline Savra marriage and family therapist | Roswell, GA. Jousline Savra Marriage and Family Therapist | Roswell, GA. https://www.jouslinesavra.com/why-communication-is-important-in-a-marriage/

Gaspard, T. (2024, June 25). How to Build Trust with Your Partner After Infidelity. The Gottman Institute. https://www.gottman.com/blog/how-to-build-trust-with-your-partner-after-infidelity/

Maxwell, T. (2023, May 3). 5 ways to set financial boundaries. Experian. https://www.experian.com/blogs/ask-experian/how-to-set-financial-bound aries/

Admin. (2023, August 31). 7 Gottman-Backed conflict resolution Strategies in Marriage. The Relationship Place. https://www.sdrelationshipplace.com/ conflict-resolution-strategies-in-marriage/

Zarch, Z. N., Marashi, S. M., & Raji, H. (2014b, October 1). The Relationship between Emotional Intelligence and Marital Satisfaction: 10-Year Outcome of Partners from Three Different Economic Levels. https://www.ncbi.nlm. nih.gov/pmc/articles/PMC4361820/

Bishop, S. (2023, June 4). 6 ways to stay calm and collected during a heated argument. Mediate.com. https://mediate.com/6-ways-to-stay-calm-and-collected-during-a-heated-argument/

Forster, D. E., Billingsley, J., Burnette, J. L., Lieberman, D., Ohtsubo, Y., &

McCullough, M. E. (2021). *Experimental evidence that apologies promote forgiveness by communicating relationship value. Scientific Reports, 11(1).* https://doi.org/10.1038/s41598-021-92373-y

Pel, J. (2023, March 25). *Beyond the relationship - Hello, love - medium. Medium.* https://medium.com/hello-love/beyond-the-relationship-e301266ae4e0

Seidman, G. (2015, January 5). *7 ways you can help your partner reach their goals. Psychology Today.* https://www.psychologytoday.com/us/blog/close-encounters/201501/7-ways-you-can-help-your-partner-reach-their-goals

Admin. (2023a, February 27). *Self care in Relationships: 6 Habits to Start building. The Relationship Place.* https://www.sdrelationshipplace.com/self-care-in-relationships/

SoulFacts. (2023, July 25). *Balancing independence and togetherness in relationships. Medium.* https://medium.com/@soul-facts/balancing-independence-and-togetherness-in-relationships-d3c3c00ad6ef

Tai, T. &. (2022, November 15). *Goal setting for couples: 10 tips to set Better goals with your partner. His & Her Money.* https://www.hisandhermoney.com/goal-setting-for-couples/

Somanathan, S. (2024, September 20). *10 visualization techniques to achieve your goals. ClickUp.* https://clickup.com/blog/visualization-techniques/

Panganiban, K. (2024, June 25). *How to have a state of the Union meeting. The Gottman Institute.* https://www.gottman.com/blog/how-to-have-a-state-of-the-union-meeting/

Comms. (2019, July 19). *10 ways to develop family rituals and traditions.* https://onefamily.ie/10-ways-to-develop-family-rituals-and-traditions/

Smith, S. (2024, October 29). *How to Prioritize your spouse in Marriage: 17 Effective ways. Marriage Advice - Expert Marriage Tips & Advice.* https://www.marriage.com/advice/marriage-fitness/ways-to-prioritize-your-spouse/

Eldemire, A. (2020, November 3). *How to set (and respect) boundaries with your spouse. Psychology Today.* https://www.psychologytoday.com/us/blog/couples-thrive/202011/how-set-and-respect-boundaries-your-spouse

Suknanan, J. (2024, February 8). *Are you and your partner unsure about how to start tracking your spending? Here are 3 budgeting apps that can help. CNBC.* https://www.cnbc.com/select/best-budgeting-apps-for-couples/

Scott, E., PhD. (2023, September 13). *18 effective stress relief strategies. Verywell Mind.* https://www.verywellmind.com/tips-to-reduce-stress-3145195

Heymstraveler, C. (2024, April 28). *5 Tips for Healthy Long-Distance*

Relationships - Hey Ms Traveler. *Hey Ms Traveler.* https://heymstraveler. com/long-distance-

Segal, J., PhD, & Robinson, L. (2024, February 5). Blended Family and Step-Parenting tips - HelpGuide.org. *HelpGuide.org.* https://www.helpguide.org/ articles/parenting-family/step-parenting-blended-families.htm

Supporting a spouse through a health challenge. (2024, June 20). *Johns Hopkins Medicine.* https://www.hopkinsmedicine.org/health/wellness-and-prevention/supporting-a-spouse-through-a-health-challenge

Taking Care of YOU: Self-Care for Family Caregivers - Family Caregiver Alliance. (2023, January 11). *Family Caregiver Alliance.* https://www.care giver.org/resource/taking-care-you-self-care-family-caregivers/

9 7 9 8 9 9 9 0 9 3 5 0 9